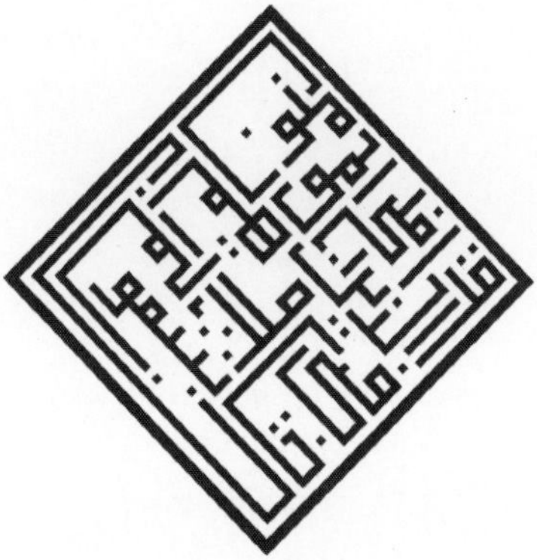

Certainly, the faithful have attained salvation
- those who are humble in their prayers,

The Holy Qur'ān (Sūrah al-Mu'minūn, 1-2)

To my wife and two children,

Amina and Ahmed,

and to all the people who are striving hard

to get close to Allah (swt),

this is my humble contribution to you.

101 WAYS TO CONCENTRATE IN PRAYER

DR. ALI AL-HILLI

FOREWORD BY SHAYKH MOHAMMAD ALI SHOMALI

SUN BEHIND THE CLOUD PUBLICATIONS LTD

Published by
Sun Behind The Cloud Publications Ltd
PO Box 15889, Birmingham, B16 6NZ

This edition first published in paperback 2014

A CIP catalogue record for this book is available from the British Library

ISBN (print): 978-1-908110-21-3
ISBN (ePUB): 978-1-908110-24-4

Printed in the United Kingdom
www.sunbehindthecloud.com
info@sunbehindthecloud.com

Contents

Transliteration Table

ء	’	ز	z	ق	q	Long vowels	
ب	b	س	s	ك	k	ا	ā
ت	t	ش	sh	ل	l	و	ū
ث	th	ص	ṣ	م	m	ي	ī
ج	j	ض	ḍ	ن	n	Short vowels	
ح	ḥ	ط	ṭ	ه	h	ـَ	a
خ	kh	ظ	ẓ	و	w	ـُ	u
د	d	ع	‘	ي	y	ـِ	i
ذ	dh	غ	gh	ة	ah		
ر	r	ف	f	ال	al		

Foreword

We have been given the opportunity to call Allah (swt), and this is a great blessing. In addition to this, we have been permitted, and indeed recommended, to call Him anytime, under any circumstance. This is the case even in situations when we may feel embarrassed to talk to Him, such as immediately after committing a blameworthy action, when we feel we have damaged our relationship with Him, making Him angry with us. Still, He is so kind that He says you can and *should* call Me. So we should be very happy and grateful for this blessing of being able to call Him despite our own situation and despite what we have done in the past, what people think about us, and what we think about ourselves. Furthermore, He has blessed us by designing and introducing to us a very effective and beautiful way of calling Him; and that is ṣalāh.

We can call Him and make our requests in any language, in different manners combined with different actions, we can praise Him in the way that we like, or understand, but the best way of calling Him is ṣalāh. In addition to being a very meaningful, articulate and structured way to call Allah (swt) that can bring order and uniformity to all Muslims, ṣalāh is a divine design which we are supposed to materialize and bring into existence.

Consider ṣalāh as a vehicle that you build in order to move, such as a plane that you make so you may fly. The design is made by Allah (swt) and the materials and parts needed for producing it are also introduced and made available by Allah (swt). You just need to engineer it through the work of your body, mind and heart.

Allah (swt) has designed ṣalāh and has recommended us to pray as much as possible. In order to ensure that we are connected to Him, at least to achieve a basic level of happiness and success in our worldly life and in the Herefter, Allah (swt) has obligated daily prayers. For higher levels of perfection, we need to say recommended prayers (nawāfil) as well.

When you pray your ṣalāh according to the requirements of sharī'ah, you are casting or producing the form of a heavenly being. Remember when Prophet 'Īsā (as) made a clay statue of a bird and he blew into it; it came to life. It was a real bird (as in the verses of the Holy Qur'ān 3:49 & 5:110). When we say our prayer according to the requirements of sharī'ah, we are making the form of the ṣalāh; like a bird made from clay, but this bird cannot fly without being given life. You need to put your soul into this. When you have presence of mind and heart in ṣalāh and put your soul into it, it gains life.

When ṣalāh gains life, it will start functioning. When ṣalāh functions, it becomes your helper and aid (Holy Qur'ān 2:45 and 153), it prevents you from committing bad actions (29:45), it acts like a ladder (mi'rāj al-mu'min) by which you can ascend and like a river that helps you to remove any impurity and darkness (*Tahdhīb al-'Aḥkām*, vol. 2, p. 238).

Now it becomes clear why ṣalāh is considered as the best action (khayr al-'amal), though our ṣalāh may not the best action. In other words, if we say our prayer properly according to instructions given by Allah (swt) then it would be the best of our deeds. The term which is commonly used in our 'aḥādīth to refer to the right attitude that enables ṣalāh to function is 'iqbāl' (to come; to arrive) which means to meet Allah (swt) with your heart and mind; that is, your soul must not be absent.

Consider this example: imagine you have an employee who works for you and you ask him to meet you every day to deliver a report. He is required to report on his commitment and loyalty to the work; the task that he has been given in the institution; his completed tasks, such as checking emails, contacting people, making payments, planning for future progress and attending meetings. In the report he has to mention that he has done all these things properly. Now imagine if that employee does not come to report at all, or he comes and gives a report like a parrot without understanding or meaning what he is saying to you, or lies by saying things that he has not done. Is this going to help? Is this going to make him closer to you? Or it is going to make you develop a bad opinion about him?

So when Allah (swt) instructs us to come to Him, five times a day, with purity and presence of heart, and say that we only worship Him and we only ask assistance from Him; we should be able to speak truthfully and mean what we say. If someone does not think about what he says, the meeting becomes fruitless. Similarly, if someone thinks about what he says and means it, but is not actually, truthfully practicing those things, the meeting becomes ineffective. But if I am able to stand before Allah (swt) in my ṣalāh and deliver my report to Him in a very truthful and honest way, with presence of heart, then I have given life to it and established it so that it can ascend towards Allah (swt) like a bird that is thrown into the air and continues flying. But ṣalāh without this is just like a statue or model. If it is thrown into the air it will plummet to the ground, becoming a danger to yourself and those around you.

According to 'aḥādīth, ṣalāh without iqbāl is not accepted. If all of it lacks iqbāl, all of it is rejected, and if part of it lacks iqbāl, that part is rejected. If our ṣalāh is dead, it would not be accepted; it would be like a plane that cannot fly or a car that cannot move. Moreover, if ṣalāh, which is supposed to be our best action, is rejected, then all our actions will be rejected. Imām al-Bāqir (as) is quoted as saying: "*The first thing that one would be questioned about is ṣalāh. If it is accepted other things will be accepted.*" (*al-Kāfī*, vol. 3, p. 268; *Tahdhīb al-'Aḥkām*, vol. 2, p. 239)

So prayer is, in a sense, a reflection of your success. It is the result of your life and every quality that you have and everything that you do. Everything about you is on display. Everything that you do is reflected in your ṣalāh.

I am very pleased to see that attention to ṣalāh is increasing in our community and in society at large. An increasing number of lectures, workshops and publications about ṣalāh emerge and more places for prayer are made available to the public. Thus, I am very happy to see the present publication by the Sun Behind the Cloud and find it timely. *101 Ways to Concentrate in Prayer* by Dr. Ali Al-Hilli, is to be welcomed by those who try to understand the significance of ṣalāh better and, in particular, want to have presence of heart during their prayer. As a humble brother, I thank both the publisher and the author, and humbly request Allah (swt) to reward them and bless this publication. I also pray that we as individuals and a community give ṣalāh its due respect and highest commitment. I hope we witness the day when we stand for ṣalāh and become immersed in conversation with Allah (swt), that nothing worldly is able to divert our attention away, and that nothing dishonest can be found in what we say to Him.

Mohammad Ali Shomali
Qum al-Muqaddasah
February 2014/ Rabī' al-thānī 1435

Preface

Prayer teaches us how to eliminate pride and live a life of inner courage. It can transport us to a higher plane, and make us become aware of a place deep inside that is absolutely silent and still, beyond the reach of time and grief. Reciting the verses of the Holy Qur'ān brings peace, enlightenment and tranquillity. The movements affect us deeply and bring us an enormous sense of emotional freedom. It is connection with the Lord. It is what we are born to do.

So, whilst we pray around 1,825 obligatory prayers a year, why do we not effectively benefit from them? Why do we not see continual progress in our spirituality and in our connection and relationship with the Almighty (swt).

The question is: are we satisfied with our prayer? Is our heart conscious of Allah and in awe of Him when we approach prayer? Are we benefitting from prayer the way it was intended?

To find out the answers to these questions, I conducted an anonymous survey over the internet and asked people to participate. The first question in the survey asked: *How would you rate your concentration in prayer from 1-10, 1 being poor and 10 being perfect?*

Results showed 68% said in the 1-5 (poor to average) range, 29% rated it from 6-7, and only 3 people rated their concentration in their prayer in the 8-10 range.

The second question asked: *If you are finding it difficult to concentrate in your prayer, why do you think that is?* 62% of the people surveyed stated that the reason why they found it difficult to concentrate was that their mind was always pre-occupied, 13% put it down to being in a hurry, 11% to weakness of faith, 7% felt that their prayer was repetitive and systematic and 5% put their lack of concentration down to tiredness when approaching the prayer. Some also gave other reasons which included: easily distracted (by children and others), lack of mental preparation before prayer, and feeling pressurised to concentrate.

The third question asked: *Have you tried ways to improve your concentration in prayer?* 83% replied in the affirmative and 17% said that they had not.

The fourth question asked: *If your answer is yes, what are those ways?* The responses included: translating the verses in one's mind as it is recited during prayer, breathing techniques, and contemplating prior to prayer.

The fifth question asked: *Do you feel your prayer is empty when you don't concentrate in your prayer?* 70% said that their prayer felt empty when they lost attention in prayer and 30% said they did not.

The final question asked: *Are you willing to try new ways to concentrate in prayer?* 98% are willing to try new ways of concentration in their prayer.

In summary, the survey showed that the majority of the people find it difficult, in most cases, to concentrate in prayer, mainly because the mind is occupied with worldly things. Consequently, they feel their prayer is empty and not submissive towards Allah (swt). However, most of them have tried new ways to improve their concentration in prayer and are willing to try other techniques to connect their heart and mind to the Almighty (swt) during prayer.

The ultimate aim of this book is to raise awareness about khushūʿ (submissiveness towards Allah) in prayer as many of us, (as shown by the above survey), are losing touch with our prayer and may have began underestimating or undermining the power of prayer. The quality of our prayer is the best indicator of the strength of our connection with our Lord. As this connection weakens, we are more likely to face problems at societal, family and personal levels. It is impossible to find someone who has complete khushūʿ in their prayer and has bad traits such as arrogance or back biting. It is equally impossible to find someone who is corrupt and devious and is fully connected with Allah (swt) during prayer. The two are incompatible.

Connection to Allah (swt) during the prayer leads to remembrance of Him outside of the prayer. Therefore, prayer with concentration is a protection against sinful acts; is a source of happiness; and strengthens our patience and perseverance. I believe that improving our khushūʿ in prayer is the key to becoming better believers and building a more integrated society as a whole, 'inshā Allāh.

On a personal note, I felt that to get closer to Allah in my prayer, I needed to go through a journey to explore various techniques to achieve this closeness to the Lord. I began my path by reading and learning from our esteemed scholars and what they report from the Holy Qurʿān and ʿaḥādīth. I also began to research and think about other methods, including some contemporary techniques that may be helpful in sustaining khushūʿ in prayer. The results of this journey are humbly presented in this book. Some comments regarding the points raised in this book are as follows.

The criteria for judging whether the points proposed in this book are helpful or not is that each method must be jurisprudentially correct, independently reviewed, realistic, viable and practical. The research results were put together from different sources, namely from the literature and scholarly (academic and religious) recommendations. Some of the points raised are new suggestions on how to concentrate in prayer. I pray that these and other points can present a different angle to focussing our heart and mind in prayer.

The points do not teach a person *how* to pray (as one can refer to the jurisprudential books for information on that), rather they suggest methods to improve our concentration and strengthen our khushūʿ in prayer. The points have been written assuming the person knows how to perform the obligatory prayers.

Some points include mustaḥab (recommended) acts to perform before, during and after prayer. They have been checked mainly against Sayid Yazdi's book as commented by Ayatollah Sistani. Please refer to your respective marjiʿ for confirmation.

Although I have attempted to select only those 'aḥādīth that are authentic, we must still practise caution when attributing 'aḥādīth to the Holy Prophet (saw) and his family. Therefore, I have written 'it is narrated' for each ḥādīth rather than 'he said'. The latter implies that we are sure of the authenticity of the 'aḥādīth, whereas the former attributes the 'aḥādīth to the narrator but with caution.

You may read through the book and apply/comprehend all the points, but eventually find only one or two points that strengthen your concentration in prayer. Either way, take your time to understand and comprehend the different methods and once you feel you are ready, then begin to apply them. You may begin by applying a few techniques and assess whether they have made any difference to your concentration during prayer. If you feel they have not made difference then you may move to the other points. However, revisit the points that may not have helped you as the time and the environment may have influenced your perception of the method. This book is meant to be continually read and used as the methods and suggestions given in this book are not just for information but for continuous practise on our journey towards Allah (swt). Indeed, the effectiveness of the points depends on the person applying them, but I pray to Allah (swt) that you will find at least one point that will help you in your journey towards the Almighty (swt).

Finally, I would like to express my gratitude and thankfulness to the Almighty, the Omnipotent and Omniscient Lord, who has given me the opportunity to serve Him and to search for ways to get closer to Him.

I am indebted to my parents who have always supported and encouraged me to work for the sake of Allah (swt), and helped me in my quest to find Him. I am grateful to my father, Dr. Walid Al-Hilli, whose teachings and guidance have been invaluable in my life.

My thanks go to Ayatollah Sayid Fadhil Milani, Shaykh Mohammad Saeed Bahmanpour, and Shaykh Mustafa Jaffar for reviewing and endorsing the book. I am grateful to Shaykh Mohammad Ali Shomali for enlightening us with his wisdom in the foreword to this book. My thanks go to my brother, Shaykh Mohammed Al-Hilli, for his support and scholarly review of the book. I am also thankful to Dr. Mojahid Najim for reviewing the book and checking the authenticity of the 'aḥādīth used; and to Dr. Muhammad Reza Fakhr Rohani who assisted with the diacritics. I am also grateful to Hussain Tahan, Hasan Al-Abadi, Yousif Al-Hilli, Dr. Ahmed Shafi, Miqdaad Versi, Hayder Jafari, Dr. Safraz Jeraj and Maria Pattinson. My thanks also go to sister Tehseen Merali from Sun Behind The Cloud Publications for her excellent editing and review of the book. May Allah (swt) reward her efforts.

Last but not least, I am forever indebted to my beloved wife, Dr. Kawther Abbas who has always had faith in my endeavours and supported me throughout the years of research and preparation for this book. Her extensive knowledge of the Islamic literature and her precise assessment of the points raised in this book have also been invaluable. Her reward is in no doubt with Allah (swt).

Finally brothers and sisters, I leave this book in your hands and pray to Allah (swt) that it can help you, as it did for me, to strengthen your concentration in prayer. Please do not forget me, my family and all the believers all around the world in your prayers.

رَبَّنَا تَقَبَّلْ مِنَّا ۖ إِنَّكَ أَنْتَ السَّمِيعُ الْعَلِيمُ

Our Lord! accept it (this service) from us; Indeed You are the All-hearing, the All-knowing. (2:127)

Ali Al-Hilli
London
February 2014/Rabīʿ al-thānī 1435

Chapter 1: Introduction

In this chapter:

- **Why do we worship Allah?**
- **What does the word ṣalāh mean?**
- **What are the benefits of prayer?**
- **Concentration in prayer**
- **Lack of concentration in prayer**
- **The science behind attention**
- **Improving concentration in prayer**

As Muslims, our spiritual enhancement and sustenance is our prayer. This prayer, or ṣalāh, is the complete submission to Allah (swt) by comprehending His greatness, beauty and absolute power through uninterrupted communication with Him. It is a time when the believer has the opportunity to reflect on his mistakes, increase his faith and strengthen his connection with the Almighty.

Prayer keeps the believer in the vicinity of Allah (swt) through continuous remembrance and obedience. If performed with presence of the heart, the prayer educates him by instilling discipline and self-restraint, keeping him away from sins, indecency and evil by purifying his heart with the clean and spiritual nourishment of the prayer. It is also the source of tranquillity and happiness and obliterates anxieties through familiarity with the Beloved.

Allah (swt) describes the characteristics of a true believer as one who performs the prayer while his heart trembles with fear and awe when He is mentioned:

إِنَّمَا الْمُؤْمِنُونَ الَّذِينَ إِذَا ذُكِرَ اللَّهُ وَجِلَتْ قُلُوبُهُمْ وَإِذَا تُلِيَتْ عَلَيْهِمْ آيَاتُهُ زَادَتْهُمْ إِيمَانًا وَعَلَىٰ رَبِّهِمْ يَتَوَكَّلُونَ

الَّذِينَ يُقِيمُونَ الصَّلَاةَ وَمِمَّا رَزَقْنَاهُمْ يُنْفِقُونَ

أُولَٰئِكَ هُمُ الْمُؤْمِنُونَ حَقًّا ۚ لَهُمْ دَرَجَاتٌ عِنْدَ رَبِّهِمْ وَمَغْفِرَةٌ وَرِزْقٌ كَرِيمٌ

The faithful are only those whose hearts tremble [with awe] when Allah is mentioned and when His signs are recited to them they increase their faith, and who put their trust in their Lord, maintain prayer and spend out of what We have provided them. It is they who are truly faithful. They shall have ranks near their Lord and a noble provision. (8: 2-4)

The reward they are granted for opening their heart to the Almighty and preserving His presence in their heart is an elevated position in Paradise. Imām al-Bāqir (as) is narrated to have said:

إنّ أوّل ما يحاسب به العبد الصلاة، فإن قبلت قبل ما سواها

"The first thing that a servant shall be reckoned for (on the Day of Judgment) shall be his prayers. If they are accepted, all his other deeds shall be accepted too."[1]

If prayer is performed with a present and illuminated heart and mind, every other action in life will be performed far away from any indecency and wrongdoing.

Why do we worship Allah?

Human beings are created with a thirst for understanding, an inborn capacity and 'fiṭrah'. Although there is no accurate translation for the word 'fiṭrah' into English, it is often translated as 'the initial disposition', 'the natural tendency of man' or "*the natural constitution (al-khilqah) with which a child is created in his mother's womb.*"[2] Allah (swt) says in the Holy Qur'ān that He has created or 'originated' people with faith, so we should maintain the prayer and keep away from polytheism:

فَأَقِمْ وَجْهَكَ لِلدِّينِ حَنِيفًا ۚ فِطْرَتَ اللَّهِ الَّتِي فَطَرَ النَّاسَ عَلَيْهَا ۚ لَا تَبْدِيلَ لِخَلْقِ اللَّهِ ۚ ذَٰلِكَ الدِّينُ الْقَيِّمُ وَلَٰكِنَّ أَكْثَرَ النَّاسِ لَا يَعْلَمُونَ مُنِيبِينَ إِلَيْهِ وَاتَّقُوهُ وَأَقِيمُوا الصَّلَاةَ وَلَا تَكُونُوا مِنَ الْمُشْرِكِينَ

So set your heart on the religion as a people of pure faith, the origination of Allah according to which He has created mankind. (There is no altering Allah's creation; that is the upright religion, but most people do not know.) Turning to him in penitence and be wary of Him, and maintain the prayer and do not be among the polytheists. (30:30-31)

The verse above also indicated that this innate nature which He has created within us cannot be altered. This means that humankind will always tend towards worship of a higher being, whether that worship is for Allah (swt), or idols such as during the pre-Islamic era, or the "idols" worshipped in the modern era. Allah (swt) says in the Holy Qur'ān:

وَمَا خَلَقْتُ الْجِنَّ وَالْإِنْسَ إِلَّا لِيَعْبُدُونِ

I did not create the jinn and the humans except that they may worship Me. (51:56)

Allah (swt) is not in need of our worship; rather we worship Him to elevate ourselves and seek guidance from Him to reach perfection. Worship is a form of self-development; the more we worship Allah, the more we develop spiritually, psychologically and socially. This must be done not just by praying, fasting and performing ḥajj, but also by taking care of our families, visiting the sick and giving charity. In fact the believers can turn their daily activities into acts of worship by purifying their intentions and sincerely seeking Allah's (swt) pleasure through these activities.

What does the word salah mean?

Many jurists and Arab litterateurs define the literal root meaning of the word ṣalāh as 'invocation'.[3] There are two forms of invocation in Islam. The first is ṣalāh, which is the prescribed daily prayer that has formal jurisprudential requirements and acts, and the second is du'ā', which is the supplicatory invocation that represents an open-ended conversation with Allah (swt) that may occur at any time and at any place.

One of the first usages of the word ṣalāh was during Prophet Ismāʿīl's time as Prophet Ibrāhīm settled a part of his offspring in Makkah to keep up prayer, which resulted in the frequent use of the word ṣalāh:

رَبَّنَا إِنِّي أَسْكَنْتُ مِنْ ذُرِّيَّتِي بِوَادٍ غَيْرِ ذِي زَرْعٍ عِنْدَ بَيْتِكَ الْمُحَرَّمِ رَبَّنَا لِيُقِيمُوا الصَّلَاةَ فَاجْعَلْ أَفْئِدَةً مِنَ النَّاسِ تَهْوِي إِلَيْهِمْ وَارْزُقْهُمْ مِنَ الثَّمَرَاتِ لَعَلَّهُمْ يَشْكُرُونَ

Our Lord! I have settled part of my descendants in a barren valley, by Your sacred House, our Lord, that they may maintain the prayer. So make the hearts of a part of the people fond of them, and provide them with fruits, so that they may give thanks. (14:37)

What are the benefits of prayer?

Prayer performed with a present heart and mind has many benefits. A few are listed below:

1. An opportunity to get closer to Allah. Allah (swt) has blessed us with many opportunities in the day to get close to Him and communicate with Him. He invites us to His presence five times a day, and wants us to reach Him by contemplating on His essence to better ourselves. Once engaged in prayer, we are in a direct relationship with the Creator who is very near, hears everything we say and responds to each request. Allah (swt) says in sūrah al-Baqarah:

وَإِذَا سَأَلَكَ عِبَادِي عَنِّي فَإِنِّي قَرِيبٌ ۖ أُجِيبُ دَعْوَةَ الدَّاعِ إِذَا دَعَانِ ۖ فَلْيَسْتَجِيبُوا لِي وَلْيُؤْمِنُوا بِي لَعَلَّهُمْ يَرْشُدُونَ

When My servants ask you about Me, [tell them that] I am indeed nearmost. I answer the supplicant's call when he calls Me. So let them respond to Me, and let them have faith in Me, so that they may fare rightly. (2:186)

If we sincerely supplicate from the depth of our heart to Allah (swt), He guarantees His response to our cry.[4] This is the manifestation of Allah's Will as the All-Knowing, the Hearer and the Responsive.

2. Keeps you away from sins. Allah (swt) says:

اتْلُ مَا أُوحِيَ إِلَيْكَ مِنَ الْكِتَابِ وَأَقِمِ الصَّلَاةَ ۖ إِنَّ الصَّلَاةَ تَنْهَىٰ عَنِ الْفَحْشَاءِ وَالْمُنْكَرِ ۗ وَلَذِكْرُ اللَّهِ أَكْبَرُ ۗ وَاللَّهُ يَعْلَمُ مَا تَصْنَعُونَ

Recite what has been revealed to you of the Book, and maintain the prayer. Indeed the prayer prevents indecencies and wrongs, and the remembrance of Allah is surely greater. And Allah knows whatever [deeds] you do. (29:45)

The prayer with a present heart and mind is one that will keep the believer in the constant remembrance of Allah (swt). Maintaining such a state all the time would make committing sins extremely difficult as the attentive heart would always be aware of the existence of Allah (swt). Prayer is a form of education and discipline; if performed properly, it should act as a shield against any indecency and evil. It trains the believer to be in a high state of submissiveness with morals that will keep him safely away from sins.

3. Sets your heart at rest. If you seek a tranquil and comfortable heart, one that is satisfied and restful, then you must always be in vicinity of Allah (swt) through His remembrance. This is emphasised twice in one verse, which indicates its importance and benefits:

الَّذِينَ آمَنُوا وَتَطْمَئِنُّ قُلُوبُهُمْ بِذِكْرِ اللَّهِ ۗ أَلَا بِذِكْرِ اللَّهِ تَطْمَئِنُّ الْقُلُوبُ

Those who have faith, and whose hearts find rest in the remembrance of Allah. Look! The hearts find rest in Allah's remembrance! (13:28)

Pooya Yazdi, in his commentary of the Holy Qur'ān, explains how the remembrance of Allah, which is the essence of prayer, frees the believer from all worries except the worry of his/her shortcomings towards his Creator:

> "Tranquillity and fear are apparently opposite to each other. A true believer seeks tranquillity in the midst of conflicting desires of the worldly life and fears when he feels that there are many shortcomings in his submission to Allah. The remembrance of Allah produces these effects simultaneously in him and sets him free from all worldly worries."[5]

Indeed the only worry we should have in our life is our shortcomings in fulfilling the duties to our Lord. Anything else is insignificant.[6]

4. Liberates you from all types of subjugation. Prayer represents a concrete manifestation of the Islamic conception of freewill. The decision to pray is one that must be made by the individual. Once engaged in prayer, he feels the essence of freedom by breaking free from the chains of family, friends and society and liberates himself to please His Lord. He sets his heart and mind to the Only One, practising his freewill with security and contentment. This servitude to Allah is the ultimate source of freedom.

5. Relaxes you and strengthens your patience. The Holy Qur'ān emphasises the connection between patience and prayer and how they are achievable only to those who are humble:

وَاسْتَعِينُوا بِالصَّبْرِ وَالصَّلَاةِ ۚ وَإِنَّهَا لَكَبِيرَةٌ إِلَّا عَلَى الْخَاشِعِينَ

And take recourse in patience and prayer, and it is indeed hard except for the humble. (2:45)

If you are about to get involved in a situation that requires patience then it is best to pray first as prayer relaxes the mind, nourishes the soul and strengthens confidence. Your connection with the everlasting Power, Allah (swt), will surely make all your hard problems and difficult complications easy.

Some exegetes report that the word sabr in this verse means fasting and thus they explain that the believer should revert to prayer and fasting in difficult and strenuous times.

In addition, the Holy Qur'ān describes the people who pray, al-muṣallīn, as those who do not become anxious when evil afflicts them, and do not become greedy and grudging when good is bestowed on them:

إِنَّ الْإِنْسَانَ خُلِقَ هَلُوعًا

إِذَا مَسَّهُ الشَّرُّ جَزُوعًا

وَإِذَا مَسَّهُ الْخَيْرُ مَنُوعًا

إِلَّا الْمُصَلِّينَ

الَّذِينَ هُمْ عَلَىٰ صَلَاتِهِمْ دَائِمُونَ

Indeed man has been created covetous: anxious when an ill befalls him and grudging when good comes his way [all are such] except the prayerful, those who are persevering in their prayers. (70:19-23)

Concentration in prayer

It is necessary to approach prayer with an unoccupied mind and a present heart filled with awe and reverence of the magnificence of the Lord. The believer must be fully aware of their worthlessness and submit to the Absolute Omnipotent in humility and humbleness.

Allah (swt) says in sūrah al-Mu'minūn:

قَدْ أَفْلَحَ الْمُؤْمِنُونَ

الَّذِينَ هُمْ فِي صَلَاتِهِمْ خَاشِعُونَ

Certainly, the faithful have attained salvation - those who are humble in their prayers. (23:1-2)

Taking a moment to ponder on the meaning of these two verses reveals the beauty in their meaning; Allah (swt) is broadcasting a joyful announcement for those who deserve the reward. He is guaranteeing success, not just to any believer but to those who, in their prayer, are submissive, humble and have a present heart and mind; those who understand the greatness, majesty and beauty of Allah (swt) and are fearful of Allah (swt). This true khushū' (also known as khushū' al-'īmān) is the reverence of the heart before Allah (swt) with humbleness, dignity and modesty as the heart trembles in the presence of the Almighty. These are the true believers as described by the Holy Qur'ān:

إِنَّمَا الْمُؤْمِنُونَ الَّذِينَ إِذَا ذُكِرَ اللَّهُ وَجِلَتْ قُلُوبُهُمْ وَإِذَا تُلِيَتْ عَلَيْهِمْ آيَاتُهُ زَادَتْهُمْ إِيمَانًا وَعَلَىٰ رَبِّهِمْ يَتَوَكَّلُونَ

الَّذِينَ يُقِيمُونَ الصَّلَاةَ وَمِمَّا رَزَقْنَاهُمْ يُنْفِقُونَ

أُولَٰئِكَ هُمُ الْمُؤْمِنُونَ حَقًّا ۚ لَهُمْ دَرَجَاتٌ عِنْدَ رَبِّهِمْ وَمَغْفِرَةٌ وَرِزْقٌ كَرِيمٌ

The faithful are only those whose hearts tremble [with awe] when Allah is mewntioned, and when His signs are recited to them, they increase their faith, and who put their trust in their Lord, maintain the prayer and spend out of what We have provided them. It is they who are truly the faithful. They shall have ranks near their Lord, forgiveness and a noble provision. (8: 2-4)

Notice in these verses Allah (swt) does not describe the true believers as those who pray, but those who *establish* the prayer; those who keep the prayer as a core and respected compartment of their daily lives. These believers do not find it difficult to concentrate and establish the connection with the Almighty during prayer (sūrah 2, verse 45) and look forward to the next prayer.

In another verse, Allah (swt) orders the believers to perform the prayer with the correct state of mind:

حَافِظُواْ عَلَى الصَّلَوَاتِ والصَّلاَةِ الْوُسْطَى وَقُومُواْ لِلّهِ قَانِتِينَ

Be watchful of your prayers, and [especially] the middle prayer, and stand in obedience to Allah. (2:238)

Great emphasis is given to the prayer that is performed with the correct state of mind. One prayer with concentration can hold far more reward than hundreds of prayers without concentration. Furthermore, the prayer of a believer is accepted according to the level of khushū' sustained during the prayer as narrated from Imām al-Ṣādiq (as):

إن من الصلاة لما يقبل نصفها وثلثها وربعها إلى العشر، وإن منها لما تلف كما يلف الثوب الخلق ويضرب بها وجه صاحبها، ومالـك مـن صـلاتك الا ما أقبلت عليه بقلبك

"As for the prayer, half of it may be accepted, or one-third, or a quarter, or one-fifth, or even one-tenth. Another prayer may be folded like an old dress, and be thrown back at the face of its owner. No part of the prayer is yours except that part which you perform with an attentive heart."[7]

A submissive believer, known as a khashi', does not merely practice humility and modesty in his prayer, but also adopts these and other forms of 'akhlāq in his daily life. Therefore, a khashi' can be distinguished from a non-khashi' not by the outward submissiveness in his prayer but by his daily actions in life, and whether these prayers have kept him away from indecency and evil as narrated by this ḥādīth from Imām al-Ṣādiq (as):

مَنْ أَحَبَّ أَنْ يَعْلَمَ أَ قُبِلَتْ صَلاَتُهُ أَمْ لَمْ تُقْبَلْ فَلْيَنْظُرْ هَـلْ مَنَعَتْـهُ صَـلاَتُهُ عَنِ الْفَحْشَآءِ وَ الْمُنْكَرِ فَبِقَدْرِ مَا مَنَعَتْهُ قُبِلَتْ مِنْهُ.

"One who desires to know if his prayer has been accepted or not, should observe if it has kept him away from indecency and evil, or not; the measure in which it has kept him away (is the measure of his prayer that) has been accepted."[8]

Lack of concentration in prayer

Concentration in prayer can be difficult, especially when our mind is engaged with other 'important' matters in life. You may relate to the times when you say *'Allāhu 'Akbar* in takbīrat al-'iḥrām, and an influx of thoughts enter your mind. It feels like a door opens up as soon as we perform takbīrat al-'iḥrām and the issues that we have been occupied with march through, and override our feeble attempts to focus solely on our Lord. A few minutes later, we start to doubt what rak'ah we are in and then may need to apply the appropriate rulings of al-shakk fī al-ṣalāh (doubt in prayer) to 'save' our prayer from becoming void (or in some cases we must repeat the prayer).

Imam Khomeini (ra), in his book *'Ādāb al-Ṣalāt*,[9] describes a beautiful analogy of the concept of thoughts appearing and disappearing during prayer. He calls it 'the bird of imagination'. The imagination (khayal), which is a natural faculty of the human mind, is like a bird that flies from one place to another. If man was to study its movements during a very short period of time (such as the time it takes to pray) he will find that the bird has moved continuously to many trivial and irrelevant places. In other words, his imagination during prayer will contain images and sensations that represent multiple non-connected and unimportant events that may have occurred in the past or might occur in the future. If you were to ask someone about their bird of imagination at the end of their prayer, you may find that they have imagined a particular scene at work, or images of people who they know or anything relating to a recent event that has occurred. What needs to be done, therefore, is not to halt our imagination during prayer, but steer our imagination towards the Almighty and His bounties. Imam Khomeini (ra) suggests *"acquiring calmness of mind, peace of soul and repose of imagination"* to help in limiting the power of the bird of imagination.

The bird of imagination also flutters recklessly outside the prayer. According to researchers, half of the time when we are engaged in doing something, our minds drift off to thoughts unrelated to what we are doing. Research conducted by Jonathan Smallwood and colleagues reports that this is probably related to what we have stored in our 'working memory'. Working memory is the mental workspace that allows us to juggle multiple thoughts simultaneously. He says:

> "Our results suggest that the sorts of planning that people do quite often in daily life – when they're on the bus, when they're cycling to work, when they're in the shower – are probably supported by working memory… Their brains are trying to allocate resources to the most pressing problems."[10]

Although they argue that mind wandering, whether conscious or not, may be an indication of underlying priorities being held in working memory, this does not mean that people with high working memories are bound to concentrate less on particular tasks.

Daniel Levinson, Smallwood's research colleague, said:

> "The bottom line is that working memory is a resource and it's all about how you use it. If your priority is to keep attention on task, you can use working memory to do that, too."[11]

Therefore adding the various methods of concentration in prayer and comprehending the importance of concentrating in prayer in our working memory is a viable way to overcome the trivial distractions we get from our working memory during prayer.

The science behind attention

Scott Scheper, in his book, *How to Get Focused*, discusses three shift phases the mind goes through while in the process of concentrating.[12] Below, the example of prayer is used to describe the phases:

Phase 1: Blood Rush Alert

When you approach prayer and perform takbīrat al-'iḥrām, blood rushes to your anterior prefrontal cortex. Within this part of the brain, sits a neurological switchboard. The switchboard alerts the brain that it is about to shift attention.

Phase 2: Find and Execute

The alert carries an electrical charge that is composed of two parts: a search query (discover neurons that will execute the prayer task) and a command (rouse the neurons once discovered). This process propels you into a mental state of prayer. If you have the ability to continue concentrating then your brain will continue in phase 2 until the end of prayer. Otherwise it will go to phase 3.

Phase 3: Disengagement

If you get distracted by either an external source (such as, children running around, loud TV or mobile phone ringing) or an internal source (such as worries and random thoughts), your mind rapidly disengages with its current praying state, and sends blood-flow back to phase 1, which then leads you to phase 2, and then when you get distracted again, you will find yourself at phase 3 again.

The method to prevent the entrance of the mind into phase 3 is to maintain sustainable attention (as compared to other types of attention such as selective and divided attention) in our prayer. This is defined as: *"a state in which a person remains cognizant despite performing or experiencing something that does not readily keep his or her attention."*[13] The person will remain consistently focused on the task at hand for as long as it lasts, from beginning to end. Some techniques and ideas to achieve sustainable attention in prayer are put forward in the following chapters. Furthermore, it is important to bear in mind that to achieve khushūʿ in prayer, mastering attention alone is not sufficient. Coupled with attention must be the presence of the heart, which will be explored further in the upcoming chapters. In this book, we will refer to this marriage of the two as concentration.

Improving concentration in prayer

Generally speaking, everyone has had some experiences in full concentration. For instance, you may notice that while watching a movie in the cinema, people are absolutely still and have given their full attention to the movie. It will take a major distraction to break their attention stream. Other examples of situations where people may be in total concentration are when they are in a very important interview or exam that is crucial to their career. These situations show the great possibility and hope of us reaching full concentration in our prayers. However, hard work, effort and practise are needed to achieve such an undoubtedly difficult task.

To sustain khushū' in our prayers, we must always strive to encompass the highest spiritual and mental concentration. We must continuously train our heart, as it is the knowing entity, to be present spiritually, and train our mind, as it is the thinking entity, to be present mentally. When we perform the latter, Scott Scheper says the brain 'rewires' itself when it improves attention. This means that our ability to concentrate improves the more we concentrate (albeit it gets slower as we grow up). When we perform the former, our heart becomes content and muṭma'inn (assured) in the presence of the Almighty. The main question that arises here is that although we know that it is possible to improve our concentration in prayer (otherwise Allah (swt) would have not ordered us to concentrate in prayer), how do we then exercise our mind and heart to concentrate in prayer?

In answer to this question, Mulla Fayd Kashani (ra) quotes a beautiful example from 'Abū Hamid al-Ghazali in Kashani's expurgation (*tahdhīb*) of the voluminous ethical work of *'Aḥyā'*. He says:

> "Its example is that of a man under a tree who wanted his thoughts to be clear (from distractions), while the noise of the sparrows on the tree (above) disturbed him. Whenever he chased them off by a stick in his hand to resume his state of contemplation, he found them return again. The following, thus, was said to him: 'Surely this kind of movement is like that of sawani (the camel that is used to draw water from the well and carry the same); and (such circular movement) shall not change. Therefore if you would like to free yourself (from this state of continual distraction) chop off the tree altogether.

> Likewise is the tree of material desires: when its branches multiply it attracts various thoughts ,the way the sparrows were attracted to the branches of the tree, and the way a fly is attracted to dirt; it would take a long time to chase it off, for indeed whenever the fly is chased away it returns back. That is why it was called 'dhubāb' (that which returns whenever it is chased). Similar is the case with imagination. And these material passions are numerous and hardly does the supplicant lack in having them. And one origin unites them: love for the world, which is the root cause of every misdeed."[14]

If we go back to the example of watching a movie, the reason people can give their full attention to the movie is not solely because the movie is interesting and enjoyable but also because they can visualise and hear the movie. For the person who is attending an interview or an exam, he gives his full attention not just because it is important for him and his career, but also because he can see and hear the interviewers. Even if their mind is occupied with other things, the interest, possible enjoyment, importance of the task and the visual and auditory interaction supersedes and takes precedence in attention. This supersession does not take place in believers who struggle in concentrating in prayer. Imam Khomeini (ra) in his book *'Ādāb al-Ṣalāt* argues that the *"degrees of submission are according to the degrees of understanding the Greatness, Majesty and Beauty"* of Allah (swt). Understanding here does not merely mean information or knowledge, but the understanding must be encompassed by our hearts, and present in every prayer. This is what is meant by 'seeing' Allah during the prayer as narrated by this Holy Prophet (saw) in this ḥādīth:

خف الله في السر كأنك تراه، فإن لم تكن تراه فإنه يراك

"Fear Allah in isolation as if you see Him; and even if you do not see Him, He still sees you."[15]

To apply this, it might be difficult to slay the tree of material desires altogether, however, we must certainly do our utmost to attempt to cut out all material desires during prayer and steer our minds and hearts towards comprehending the greatness, majesty and beauty of Allah (swt).

Conclusion

Prayer, or ṣalāh, is the journey towards the recognition of Allah (swt). As this recognition is infinite, prayer has been made obligatory for all believers until their last breath. Once the believer tastes the sweetness of this prayer, he will begin recognising the Greatness and Omnipotence of the Lord. However, recognition is impossible without reverence and submissiveness towards the Almighty. It is narrated from Imām al-Ṣādiq (as) that he said:

والله إنه ليأتي على الرجل خمسون سنة وما قبل الله منه صلاة واحدة،
فأي شيء أشد من هذا؟ !والله إنكم لتعرفون من جيرانكم وأصحابكم من
لو كان يصلي لبعضكم ما قبلها منه لاستخفافه بها، إن الله لايقبل إلا
الحسن فكيف يقبل ما يستخف به؟

"By Allah, it is possible that a person lives for fifty years and not even a single prayer of his is accepted. Is there anything harder and more painful than this? By Allah, you will know from your neighbours and your friends that if you talk to them in the same manner as you talk in your prayer, they will not answer you and think you are ridiculing them. Allah does not accept unless it's (prayer) excellent, so how do you expect Him to accept it if it's ridiculed (prayer)?"[16]

Therefore, it is vital for all believers to continuously attempt to strengthen their concentration in prayer by synchronising the mind with the heart and soul. With the challenges and difficulties of daily life, this task is by no means easy. However, *"Verily with every difficulty there is ease", "Verily with every difficulty there is ease."* (94:5-6)

Endnotes

1. al-Kulaynī, *al-Kāfī*, vol. 3, p.268.
2. Ibn Manẓūr, *Lisān al-'Arab Dictionary.*
3. Like *al-Ṣiḥāh al-Lughah* Arabic dictionary.
4. All du'ā' are answered if supplicated sincerely, even if the answers are delayed, or not what we expect.
5. Pooya Yazdi, *Commentary of the Holy Qur'ān,* Commentry on sūrah al-Ra'd, verse 28, [http://quran.al-islam.org] 18/03/2014.
6. Fulfilling duties to Allah is done in various forms (including working to earn a living). Things that do not satisfy and please Allah (swt) are irrelevant.
7. al-Majlisī, *Biḥār Al-Anwār*, vol. 79, p.305.
8. al-Ṭabrasī, *Majma' al-Bayān*, vol. 8. p.29.
9. Khomeini, *'Ādāb al-Ṣalāt*: The Disciplines of the Prayer, Discourse one, Chapter 11.
10. D. Levinson, J. Smallwood, R. Davidson. The Persistence of Thought: Evidence for a Role of Working Memory in the Maintenance of Task-Unrelated Thinking, *Psychol Sci.* vol. 23, p. 375–380. 2012.
11. Ibid.
12. S, Scheper, *How to get Focussed*, Part I, p.26.
13. See [http://www.wisegeek.com/what-is-concentration.htm] 19/03/2014.
14. Kashani, *al-Mahajjah al-Bayḍā'*, vol 1, p.376.
15. al-Barqī, *al-Maḥāsīn,* vol. 1, p.3.
16. al-Kulaynī, *al-Kāfī*, vol. 3, p. 269.

Chapter 2: The Prerequisites

To establish a connection to the Almighty, we must work hard to build strong foundations of our faith. These foundations are called 'The Prerequisites', as without them, it is impossible to concentrate in prayer.[1]

In this chapter:

1. Increase your ma'rifah of Allah (swt)
2. Live your life as a submissive believer and refrain from committing sins
3. Control your desires
4. Practice patience
5. Limit your interaction with worldly attachments
6. Assess yourself on a regular basis
7. Learn the jurisprudential rulings
8. Humble yourself before Allah

1- Increase your ma'rifah of Allah (swt)

An essential prerequisite to concentration in prayer is to know Allah (swt) accurately; to know Who it is we are communicating with and Who we are beseeching. Searching for this inner knowledge will help us submit to Him and be in His vicinity while in prayer. Allah (swt) says in the Holy Qur'ān:

أَمَّنْ هُوَ قَانِتٌ آنَاءَ اللَّيْلِ سَاجِدًا وَقَائِمًا يَحْذَرُ الْآخِرَةَ وَيَرْجُو رَحْمَةَ رَبِّهِ ۗ قُلْ هَلْ يَسْتَوِي الَّذِينَ يَعْلَمُونَ وَالَّذِينَ لَا يَعْلَمُونَ ۗ إِنَّمَا يَتَذَكَّرُ أُولُو الْأَلْبَابِ

Is he who supplicates in the watches of the night, prostrating and standing, apprehensive of the Hereafter and expecting the mercy of his Lord...? Say, 'Are those who know equal to those who do not know?' Only those who possess intellect take admonition. (39:9)

Indeed, those who have knowledge and those who lack it are not alike. Those who have the *inner* knowledge of Allah (swt) will have their heart illuminated with light and their soul nourished with certainty and confidence in His existence. They have the ability to distinguish between ḥaqq (truth) and the bāṭil (falsehood),[2] and fear Allah (swt) in every step of their life. The knowledge teaches them the best of 'akhlāq (ethics) and to worship Allah (swt) with complete submissiveness and reverence. This knowledge gives them happiness and prosperity in this life and the next. The difference between *true* knowledge and any other knowledge is that the true knowledge of Allah is gained not only from reading books, but through other sources that enlighten the heart and soul in Allah's existence as well.

What are these sources, then, and how can we use them

to penetrate this knowledge into our hearts? The answer to this question requires detailed and in-depth explanations, and individual efforts to ponder and reflect; however, the following suggestions will hopefully provide indications towards this great knowledge.[3]

a. Try to comprehend Allah's Divine Unity (tawḥīd) by negating any kind of limitations or attributes from Him, as narrated by Imām al-Riḍhā (as):

إن أول عبادة الله معرفته. وأصل معرفته توحيده. ونظام توحيده نفي

الصفات عنه ،لشهادة العقول أن كل صفة وموصوف مخلوق

"The very first step to Allah's worship is to attain inner knowledge of Him, and the origin of attaining inner knowledge of Allah is through His Divine Unity. The very basis of His Divine Unity is to negate any kind of limitations from Him, since the intellects are able to witness that every being is created with limitations."[4]

To negate any kind of limitation from Allah (swt), we must understand that His essence cannot be comprehended, He is not limited by time or space and, as limited beings, we cannot comprehend what is limitless. Therefore, to know Allah we can only know Him through His attributes and not His Essence. His attributes, both affirmative (including Omniscience and Omnipotence) and negative (including the fact that He is unseen and He is without partner) are unique and peerless as He is the only Creator. Only with such belief can we attain inner knowledge of Allah.[5]

b. Believing that the Holy Qur'ān is the ultimate source of true knowledge as Allah (swt) says in the Holy Qur'ān:

ذَٰلِكَ الْكِتَابُ لَا رَيْبَ ۛ فِيهِ ۛ هُدًى لِلْمُتَّقِينَ

This is the Book, there is no doubt in it, a guidance to the Godwary. (2:2)

This book of knowledge should not be read for the sake of attaining and storing knowledge, but to comprehend and transform this knowledge into what we can act upon with wisdom and piety. The Holy Qur'ān was revealed to all mankind, and thus its powerful guidance and teachings can penetrate into even a layperson's heart and transform into wisdom. Mankind has been bestowed with such a noble book of knowledge that should be read on a daily basis in order to sail in the voyage of the ma'rifah of the Author of this Holy Book. Allah (swt) says in the Holy Qur'ān:

قُلْ لَئِنِ اجْتَمَعَتِ الْإِنْسُ وَالْجِنُّ عَلَىٰ أَنْ يَأْتُوا بِمِثْلِ هَٰذَا الْقُرْآنِ لَا يَأْتُونَ بِمِثْلِهِ وَلَوْ كَانَ بَعْضُهُمْ لِبَعْضٍ ظَهِيرًا

Say, 'Should all humans and jinn rally to bring the like of this Qur'ān, they will not bring the like of it, even if they assisted one another.' (17:88)

c. Sincere supplication to Allah (swt) undoubtedly assists in the path to knowing Allah as, through our invocation, we strengthen our relationship with our Lord and talk to Him freely with no mediators or helpers. This free communication releases any arrogance and raises our awareness of Allah (swt). Therefore, the people who hold the true knowledge of Allah (swt) are the supplicants that invoke Him at the time of distress, affliction and hope:

تَتَجَافَىٰ جُنُوبُهُمْ عَنِ الْمَضَاجِعِ يَدْعُونَ رَبَّهُمْ خَوْفًا وَطَمَعًا وَمِمَّا رَزَقْنَاهُمْ يُنْفِقُونَ

Their sides vacate their beds to supplicate their Lord in fear and hope, and they spend out of what We have provided them. (32:16)

d. Remembrance of Allah (swt) and continious presence with Him, leads to true knowledge of Allah (swt):

الَّذِينَ آمَنُوا وَتَطْمَئِنُّ قُلُوبُهُم بِذِكْرِ اللَّهِ ۗ أَلَا بِذِكْرِ اللَّهِ تَطْمَئِنُّ الْقُلُوبُ

...who have faith, and whose hearts find rest in the remembrance of Allah. Look! The hearts find rest in Allah's remembrance! (13:28)

Comprehending the true knowledge of Allah therefore is through the presence of Allah (swt) in the soul and the heart, as the soul will not be shaken by any false knowledge that can trick the heart into disbelief.

e. Knowing ourselves; where we came from, where we are going, and what we are like today, is core to knowing Allah (swt). Self-knowledge leads us to knowledge of Allah and ignoring our true self will cause us to forget Allah, as the Qur'ānic verse reminds us:

وَمَا أُبَرِّئُ نَفْسِي ۚ إِنَّ النَّفْسَ لَأَمَّارَةٌ بِالسُّوءِ إِلَّا مَا رَحِمَ رَبِّي ۚ إِنَّ رَبِّي غَفُورٌ رَّحِيمٌ

And do not be like those who forget Allah, so He makes them forget their own souls. It is they who are the transgressors. (59:19)

Purification of the self and removing all layers of filth will allow you to be able to receive His light (nūr) in your heart and illuminate your heart with His presence.

f. Understanding the soul: The soul, or nafs, has several aspects, which have been described in the Holy Qur'ān. Understanding and examining these aspects within our souls is a crucial stepping stone to building our faith:

Al-nafs al-'ammārah bi al-sū' (the soul that is inclined towards evil). The believer must always be in constant battle against this aspect of the soul, which is trying to satisfy its desires and the material aspects of this life. Prophet Yūsuf (as) describes this soul in sūrah Yūsuf:

وَمَا أُبَرِّئُ نَفْسِي ۚ إِنَّ النَّفْسَ لَأَمَّارَةٌ بِالسُّوءِ إِلَّا مَا رَحِمَ رَبِّي ۚ إِنَّ رَبِّي غَفُورٌ رَحِيمٌ

Yet I do not absolve my [own carnal] soul, for the [carnal] soul indeed prompts [men] to evil, except inasmuch as my Lord has mercy. Indeed my Lord is all-Forgiving, all-Merciful. (12:53)

Al-nafs al-lawwāmah (the self-reproaching or accusing soul). This aspect of the soul reproaches itself for succumbing to falsehood and going astray from the Right Path. Allah (swt) swears by this aspect of the soul:

وَلَا أُقْسِمُ بِالنَّفْسِ اللَّوَّامَةِ

And I swear by the self-blaming soul! (75:2)

Attempt to strengthen your nafs al-lawwāmah by watching over yourself during the day (murāqabah) and bringing yourself to account during the night (muḥāsabah)

Al-nafs al-muṭma'innah (the tranquil soul). This is the highest stage of the soul, where all believers should aspire to reach. It is the soul that easily distinguishes between truth (ḥaqq) and falsehood (bāṭil) and one that fully submits to Allah (swt). Allah mentions this soul in the Holy Qur'ān:

يَا أَيَّتُهَا النَّفْسُ الْمُطْمَئِنَّةُ ۚ ارْجِعِي إِلَىٰ رَبِّكِ رَاضِيَةً مَرْضِيَّةً ۚ فَادْخُلِي فِي عِبَادِي ۚ وَادْخُلِي جَنَّتِي

'O soul at peace! Return to your Lord, pleased, pleasing! Then enter among My servants! And enter My Paradise!' (89:27-30)

2- Live your life as a submissive believer and refrain from committing sins

Some will argue that it is difficult to live the life of the prophets and the Imāms of Ahl al-Bayt (as); a life that is spent in constant remembrance of Allah, fearing Him in every action and being fully aware of His existence in every moment. This is supported with the fact that unlike the prophets and Imāms of Ahl al-Bayt (as), we are fallible and with the whispers of the Shayṭān, it is difficult to maintain submissiveness in every action in life. However, the latter obstacles should not be a hindrance in setting our path towards obeying Allah (swt) in every action we perform, amid the challenges involved. Allah (swt) says in the Holy Qur'ān:

وَأَنْ لَيْسَ لِلْإِنْسَانِ إِلَّا مَا سَعَىٰ

وَأَنَّ سَعْيَهُ سَوْفَ يُرَىٰ

And that nothing belongs to man except what he strives for, and that he will soon be shown his endeavour. (53:39-40)

In fact, the following narration from Prophet Muḥammad (saw) goes further and says that if you do not live your life as a pious person, your worship will not be accepted, even if you try as hard as possible to better your prayer and fasting:

وأعلم أنكم لو صليتم حتى تكونوا كالحنايا وصمتم حتى تكونوا كالأوتار

ما ينفعكم ذلك إلا بورع

"If you were to pray so much that you (bent over) as arches and fast so much that you become [as thin as strings], Allah would not accept any of it unless it was accompanied by piety."[6]

Therefore, in every action that we do, whether it's at work, or in society or with family and friends, we must do it with full awareness and submission to Allah (swt). Surely by doing so, we will refrain from committing any sins and thus maintain a pure and present heart in our prayer.

Some recommendations on how to live as a true believer of Allah are given in the first eleven verses of sūrah al-Mu'minūn (The Believer):

قَدْ أَفْلَحَ الْمُؤْمِنُونَ

الَّذِينَ هُمْ فِي صَلَاتِهِمْ خَاشِعُونَ

وَالَّذِينَ هُمْ عَنِ اللَّغْوِ مُعْرِضُونَ

وَالَّذِينَ هُمْ لِلزَّكَاةِ فَاعِلُونَ

وَالَّذِينَ هُمْ لِفُرُوجِهِمْ حَافِظُونَ

إِلَّا عَلَىٰ أَزْوَاجِهِمْ أَوْ مَا مَلَكَتْ أَيْمَانُهُمْ فَإِنَّهُمْ غَيْرُ مَلُومِينَ

فَمَنِ ابْتَغَىٰ وَرَاءَ ذَٰلِكَ فَأُولَٰئِكَ هُمُ الْعَادُونَ

وَالَّذِينَ هُمْ لِأَمَانَاتِهِمْ وَعَهْدِهِمْ رَاعُونَ

وَالَّذِينَ هُمْ عَلَىٰ صَلَوَاتِهِمْ يُحَافِظُونَ

أُولَٰئِكَ هُمُ الْوَارِثُونَ

الَّذِينَ يَرِثُونَ الْفِرْدَوْسَ هُمْ فِيهَا خَالِدُونَ

Certainly, the faithful have attained salvation; those who are humble in their prayers, who avoid vain talk, who carry out their [duty of] zakāt, who guard their private parts (except from their spouses or their slave women, for then they are not blameworthy; but whoever seeks [anything] beyond that —it is they who are transgressors), and those who keep their trusts and covenants, and who are watchful of their prayers. It is they who will be the inheritors, who shall inherit Paradise, and will remain in it [forever]. (23:1-11)

Briefly, these verses describe the following attributes of a true believer:

- Those who concentrate humbly (defined as khushūʿ, see Chapter One) in prayer.
- Those believers who avoid the places where profanity is spoken or where there is useless or harmful talk such as gossip, backbiting and slander.
- Those believers that help in fundraising for charitable projects, such as for orphans, the people and Islamic institutions.
- Those male and female believers who guard their chastity and avoid committing forbidden sexual acts. The best way to ensure this is through healthy marriages.
- Those believers who, if they agree to keep or do something for another person, be it a secret or a will, stand by their agreement and keep the covenant.
- Those who continuously observe the prayer at the right time, place and, if possible, in congregation.

The list of attributes begins with concentration in prayer and ends with continuously observing this prayer. This illustrates the importance of prayer to a true believer and, if it is continuously observed with concentration, then the believer is on the correct path to pleasing the Lord.

3- Control your desires

Resisting temptation and controlling desires is an excellent way to facilitate greater concentration in prayer. For instance, by lowering our gaze and not looking at forbidden things, our mind will become clear of any images that could disrupt our imagination and concentration. More importantly, the mind will be spiritually pure and ready to face Allah (swt) with a clear conscience. Allah (swt) commands us in sūrah 24, to lower our gaze as this will serve to purify both our hearts and minds:

قُلْ لِلْمُؤْمِنِينَ يَغُضُّوا مِنْ أَبْصَارِهِمْ وَيَحْفَظُوا فُرُوجَهُمْ ۚ ذَٰلِكَ أَزْكَىٰ لَهُمْ ۗ إِنَّ اللَّهَ خَبِيرٌ بِمَا يَصْنَعُونَ

Tell the faithful men to cast down their looks and to guard their private parts. That is more decent for them. Allah is indeed well aware of what they do. (24:30)

It is narrated from Imām ʿAlī (as) that he said:

إِنَّمَا أَخَافُ عَلَيْكُمُ اثْنَتَيْنِ: إِتِّبَاعَ الهَوَى وَطُولَ الأَمَلِ. أَمَّا اتِّبَاعُ الهَوَى فَإِنَّهُ يَصُدُّ عَنِ الحَقِّ وَأَمَّا طُولُ الأَمَلِ فَيُنْسِي الآخِرَةَ

"I am apprehensive for you on account of two things: submission to desire and cherishing of inordinate hope. As to desire, it prevents one from ḥaqq (truth, righteousness, God); and as to inordinate hope, it makes man oblivious of the Hereafter."[7]

4- Practice patience

Patience is one of the most important characteristics of a submissive believer in prayer. Allah says in the Holy Qur'ān:

يَا أَيُّهَا الَّذِينَ آمَنُوا اسْتَعِينُوا بِالصَّبْرِ وَالصَّلَاةِ ۚ إِنَّ اللَّـهَ مَعَ الصَّابِرِينَ

O you who have faith! Take recourse in patience and prayer; indeed Allah is with the patient. (2:153)

This verse highlights the relationship between patience and prayer as Allah (swt) instructs those who believe to seek assistance through this combination of acts. This is because prayer needs patience and patience needs prayer.

روي أن علياً (عليه السلام) : «كَانَ إِذَا أَهالَهُ أَمْرٌ فَزِعٌ قَامَ إِلى الصَّلاَةِ ثُمَّ تَلاَ هذِهِ الآية :﴿وَاسْتَعِينُوا بِالصَّبْرِ وَالصَّلاةِ...﴾

It is narrated that whenever Imām 'Alī (as) had a worrying or difficult situation, he would retreat to prayer, and then recite the verse 2:153 quoted above.[8]

It is important to note that the patience referred to in the Holy Qur'ān does not entail enduring misery and hardship or accepting humiliation, but resisting against temptations to commit sins. True patience is having inner contentment and being thankful to Allah despite any misfortunes. Imām 'Alī (as) narrates three types of patience from his teacher, Prophet Muḥammad (saw):

الصَّبْرُ ثَلاثَةٌ: صَبْرٌ عِنْدَ المُصِيبَةِ وَصَبْرٌ عَلَى الطَّاعَةِ وَصَبْرٌ عَنِ المَعْصِيَةِ. فَمَنْ صَبَرَ عَلَى المُصِيبَةِ حَتَّى يَرُدَّهَا بِحُسْنِ عَزَائِهَا كَتَبَ اللهُ لَهُ ثَلاثَمِائَةِ دَرَجَةٍ: مَا بَيْنَ الدَّرَجَةِ إِلَى الدَّرَجَةِ كَمَا بَيْنَ السَّمَاءِ إِلَى الأَرْضِ. وَمَنْ صَبَرَ عَلَى الطَّاعَةِ كَتَبَ اللهُ لَهُ سِتَّمِائَةِ دَرَجَةٍ مَا بَيْنَ الدَّرَجَةِ إِلَى الدَّرَجَةِ كَمَا بَيْنَ تُخُومِ الأَرْضِ

إِلَى العَرْشِ. وَمَنْ صَبَرَ عَنِ المَعْصِيَةِ كَتَبَ اللهُ لَهُ تِسْعَمِائَةِ دَرَجَةٍ مَا بَيْنَ الدَّرَجَةِ إِلَى الدَّرَجَةِ كَمَا بَيْنَ تُخُومِ الأَرْضِ إِلَى مُنْتَهَى العَرْشِ

"Patience is of three kinds: patience at the time of affliction, patience in regard to obedience, and patience in regard to disobedience. One who bears patiently with affliction, resisting it with a fair consolation, God writes for him three hundred degrees (of sublimity), the elevation of one degree over another being like the distance between earth and heavens. And one who is patient in regard to obedience, God writes for him six hundred degrees (of sublimity), the elevation of one degree over another being like the distance between the earth's depths and the Throne (al-'arsh). And one who is patient in regard to disobedience, God writes for him nine hundred degrees (of sublimity), the elevation of one degree over another being like the distance between the earth's depths and the furthest frontiers of the Throne."[9]

5- Limit interaction with worldly attachments

Interaction with worldly matters can continuously occupy the mind and corrupt the prayer. These include thinking too much about work, wasting time on social networking sites, watching too much television, having senseless conversations, interacting with groups that gossip and backbite, etc. Allah (swt) says in the Holy Qur'ān:

اعْلَمُوا أَنَّمَا الْحَيَاةُ الدُّنْيَا لَعِبٌ وَلَهْوٌ وَزِينَةٌ وَتَفَاخُرٌ بَيْنَكُمْ وَتَكَاثُرٌ فِي الْأَمْوَالِ وَالْأَوْلَادِ ۖ كَمَثَلِ غَيْثٍ أَعْجَبَ الْكُفَّارَ نَبَاتُهُ ثُمَّ يَهِيجُ فَتَرَاهُ مُصْفَرًّا ثُمَّ يَكُونُ حُطَامًا ۖ وَفِي الْآخِرَةِ عَذَابٌ شَدِيدٌ وَمَغْفِرَةٌ مِنَ اللَّهِ وَرِضْوَانٌ ۚ وَمَا الْحَيَاةُ الدُّنْيَا إِلَّا مَتَاعُ الْغُرُورِ

Know that the life of this world is just play and diversion, and glitter, and mutual vainglory among you and covetousness for wealth and children - like the rain whose vegetation impresses the farmer; then it withers and you see it turn yellow, then it becomes chaff, while in the Hereafter there is a severe punishment and forgiveness from Allah and His pleasure; and the life of this world is nothing but the wares of delusion. (57:20)

If we convert our conversations from talking about people, money and materialistic issues, to talking about how to become better people, the Herefter and non-materialistic issues, then we have taken a step closer to achieving presence of the heart in prayer. It is narrated from Imām 'Alī (as):

مثل الدنيا كمثل الحية ما ألين مسها وفي جوفها السم الناقع، يحذرها الرجل العاقل ويهوى إليها الصبي الجاهل

"The example of the world is like a snake. It is soft to the touch but its inside is full of venom. A wise and intelligent man (one who fears the Lord) keeps on guard from it and an ignorant person is attracted towards it."[10]

6- Assess yourself on a regular basis

Self-examining on a regular basis is a spiritually uplifting exercise that will help achieve concentration in prayer. It is narrated from Imām al-Kāẓim (as) that he said:

ليس منا من لم يحاسب نفسه في كل يوم فإن عمل حسناً استزاد الله وإن عمل سيئاً استغفر الله منه وتاب إليه.

"He who does not call himself to account everyday is not one of us. When he does so, he must ask Allah for more if he notices that he has done a good deed, and if he notices that he has committed an evildoing, he must seek Allah's forgiveness and must repent to Him."[11]

Try to find a regular time every day[12] to ponder on how the day unfolded and examine your actions critically. This should be done alone and without the interference or interaction of a second person. The best practice is to be honest with yourself; identify your weaknesses one by one and find solutions to it. For example, if there are some defects in your worship, ask Allah (swt) sincerely for forgiveness and improvement of the defects. If you became angry for instance, especially with a family member, release the arrogance in yourself and apologise to the person you were angry with.

The main aim of self assessment is to continually progress for the better and not to allow your faith to stagnate. It is paramount to make time to perform this powerful exercise on a regular basis. Once you begin you will realise the improvements it has made to your life, prayer and faith, 'inshā Allāh.

7- Learn the jurisprudential rulings

In order to focus on the inner meaning of the prayer, it is wise to have grasped all the jurisprudential rulings of wuḍū and prayer. The main reason for this is so you are confident that your prayer is performed according to the jurisprudential rulings and your mind is clear to focus on the spirituality of the prayer rather than how to pray. For instance, you may forget to recite the Holy Qur'ān quietly during ẓuhr and 'aṣr prayers.[13] If you realised later on during prayer that you have made a mistake, and you did not know the rulings how to correct it, your mind may begin to be occuplied with thoughts about the validity of the prayers rather than focussing on the connection with Allah (swt). If however you are aware of the rulings in this regard, you are confident that the prayer is valid as the loud recitation was done unintentionally.[14]

It is therefore advisable to read all the jurisprudential rulings regarding prayer by the 'ālim you follow. You may like to seek a scholar or a learned person to check and witness you perform wuḍū and prayer.

8- Humble yourself before Allah

As humans, we often reveal our selfish nature and pride in our power as this gives us an advantage over others. However, the submissive believer in Allah (swt) abandons pride, arrogance and feelings of self-sufficiency and stands humbled, meek and submissive before his Lord. This should be the natural behaviour of the believer in all aspects of his life, from work to family life and social activities. Only through a humble attitude can the believer get closer to Allah (swt) through his prayers. Allah (swt) says in the Holy Qur'ān:

ادْعُوا رَبَّكُمْ تَضَرُّعًا وَخُفْيَةً ۚ إِنَّهُ لَا يُحِبُّ الْمُعْتَدِينَ

Supplicate your Lord, beseechingly and secretly. Indeed He does not like the transgressors. (7:55)

The believer must be humble enough not to see themselves above others. This earnestness prepares the ground for spiritual progress. The first condition for the acceptance of prayer is humility before the Lord according to the ḥadīth al-qudsī as narrated by Imām al-Ṣādiq (as):

إنما أقبل الصلاة ممن تواضع لعظمتي، ويكف نفسه عن الشهوات من أجلي، ويقطع نهاره بذكري، ولا يتعاظم على خلقي، ويطعم الجائع، ويكسو العاري، ويرحم المصاب، ويؤوي الغريب، فذلك يشرق نوره مثل الشمس، وأجعل له في الظلمات نورا وفي الجهالة علما، وأكلأه بعزتي، وأستحفظه بملائكتي، يدعوني فألبيه، ويسألني فاعطيه، فمثل ذلك عندي كمثل جنات الفردوس، لا تيبس ثمارها، ولا تتغير عن حالها

"I only accept the prayer of one who has humbled himself to My Majesty, has refrained himself from carnal desires for My sake;

who passes his day with My remembrance, does not act haughty over My creation, feeds the hungry, clothes the undressed, shows compassion to the afflicted and shelters the stranger. The light of such a person will shine like the sun and I shall grant him light in darkness and knowledge in ignorance. I will preserve him with My honour and guard him with My angels. When he calls Me, I will answer him, when he asks Me, I will grant him. His example is like the gardens of Paradise, where no fruit ever becomes dry and whose state never changes."[15]

Conclusion

The prerequisites mentioned in this chapter are part of a continual quest to gain proximity to Allah (swt). They are not points on a list that can be checked off and marked as 'completed' or obligations that are 'fulfilled'. Rather, each prerequisite has degrees, such as degrees of knowledge and patience; they must be constantly worked on, and are a part of our daily struggle as believers. Some might argue that the prerequisites mentioned are sufficient to attain full concentration in prayer, as what follows would arise naturally within the heart of a believer. However, the best way to build our relationship with the Almighty (swt) is to constantly build our true knowledge of Him, through the Holy Qur'ān, humbling ourselves before Him, whilst patiently keeping away from indecency, sin and attachment to the world, and at the same time gaining a better insight into the prayer and what Allah (swt) loves. This will be discussed in the chapters that follow.

Endnotes

1. The prerequisites mentioned in this chapter are part of a larger, more extensive field of research. It is therefore, beyond the scope of this book to extensively analyse each point.
2. People who distinguish between ḥaqq and bāṭil are known as al-Furqān.
3. For further reading into the entities of the soul and the knowledge of Allah (mari'fah), please refer to book *Self-Knowledge* by Dr. Mohammad Ali Shomali.
4. al-Ṣadūq, *al-Tawḥīd*, p. 34.
5. For further reading, please refer to *Nahj al-Balāghah*, Sermon 1.
6. al-Ṭabrasī, *Makārim al-'akhlāq*. p. 468.
7. al-Kulaynī, *al-Kāfī*, vol. 2, p. 336.
8. Ibid vol. 3, p. 480.
9. Ibid, vol. 2, p. 91.
10. Ibid, vol. 2, p. 136.
11. Ibid, vol. 2, p. 453.
12. If that is difficult then attempt once a week or even once a month.
13. Jurisprudential rulings say that the Holy Qur'ān recitations at ẓuhr and 'aṣr prayers need to be recited quietly.
14. Refer to the 'ālim you follow for his ruling on this issue.
15. al-Barqī, *al-Maḥāsin*, vol. 1, p. 15.

Chapter 3: The Preparation

There is a temptation when it comes to prayer, to simply state the takbīrat al-'iḥrām and begin as soon as possible. Yet, much like any important meeting, adequate preparation, from your appearance to your mind-set, is essential to the success of the meeting with your Lord.

In this chapter:

9. Avoid eating just prior to prayer
10. Avoid strenuous activities
11. Relieve yourself
12. Concentrate in your wuḍū (ablution)
13. Contemplate on the philosophy of wuḍū at each step and perform the recommended acts
14. Avoid excessive doubting in wuḍū
15. Give importance to cleanliness and tidiness
16. Wear appropriate clothing
17. Put on perfume before prayer
18. Choose a quiet and comfortable place to worship
19. Plan which sūrah to recite in advance
20. Contemplate on the creation of Allah (swt)
21. Relax your mind

22. Treat this prayer as if it is your last
23. Write down your thoughts and worries
24. Comprehend the philosophy of facing Makkah
25. Find Allah in your heart and stand in front of Him with piety
26. Identify factors that distract you in prayer and eliminate them
27. Complete unfinished tasks
28. Recite the 'adhān (call for prayer)
29. Perform sujūd between 'adhān and 'iqāmah
30. Recite the 'iqāmah
31. Recite du'ā after 'iqāmah
32. Recite du'ā before takbīrat al-'iḥrām
33. Imagine you are standing in front of Allah on the Day of Judgment

9- Avoid eating just prior to prayer

Excessive eating prior to prayer is one of the causes of inattention in prayer as the believer will inevitably feel uncomfortable and full. If you are hungry at the time of prayer, it is recommended to eat something light.

It is narrated from Imām al-Ṣādiq (as):

إن البطن ليطغى من أكله. وأقرب ما يكون العبد من الله إذا خف بطنه،

وأبغض ما يكون العبد من الله إذا امتلأ بطنه

"The stomach transgresses under the influence of food intake (over-eating). The nearest situation between the Almighty and his servant is when the stomach is light and the worst situation is when his stomach is full."[1]

10- Avoid strenuous activities

Taking part in tiring activities just before prayer can negatively affect our concentration. For instance, if a believer decides to play football shortly before the time of prayer, once he approaches the prayer, his body is unlikely to be in an appropriate state to concentrate and submit to Allah (swt). Exercise is undoubtedly important for the body, but it can result in fatigue that ultimately leads to feeling too exhausted to carry on. It is best therefore to avoid performing such physical activities just prior to prayers.

11- Relieve yourself

It is recommended to use the bathroom prior to wuḍū and prayer:

a. This is so we may find rest from the burden of impurities and empty ourselves of grossness and filth.

b. So the sensation of wanting to relieve yourself is avoided and a person can give his undivided attention to his prayer.

c. This will also help to maintain our state of wuḍū at all times, which is mustaḥab.

12- Concentrate in your wudu (ablution)

Wuḍū, or ablution, is a practice that is usually given little attention as it is performed many times daily. It is seen as a routine washing exercise; an inconvenient though necessary obstacle to the correct performance of prayers. If we contemplate the verses of the Holy Qur'ān and the 'aḥādīth, however, it is clear that the process of wuḍū has immense spiritual significance and, if performed correctly and with pure intentions, it is the greatest method of preparing oneself for prayer. The following are some of the spiritual significances that could help the believer in his concentration in wuḍū:[2]

- As you approach the water to perform the wuḍū, approach it as if you are proceeding to Allah's mercy and forgiveness. Purification of sins due to His mercy and forgiveness is synonymous with the purification of outer filths by water.

- While you wash away physical dirt during wuḍū, purify and clear your heart and mind from all impurities, in the way the water's purity and cleanliness removes the filth and dirt from the body.

- As you lift the water to perform wuḍū, pause for a second or two and look at the clarity of the water. As you begin washing, examine your heart and ask yourself: *"is my heart as clear as this water?"*

- In the following narration from Imām al-Riḍhā (as), a link is made between washing the different parts of the body during wuḍū and prayer:

انما أمر بالوضوء ليكون العبد طاهرا اذا قام بين يدي الجبّار وعند مناجاته ايّاه مطيعا له فيما أمر نقيّا من الارجاس والنجاسة مع ما فيه من ذهاب الكسل وطرد النعاس وتزكية الفؤاد للقيام بين يدي الجبّار. وانّما وجب على الوجه واليدين والرأس والرجلين لان العبد اذا قام بين يدي الجبار فانما يكشف من جوارحه ويظهر ما وجب به الوضوء وذلك أنه بوجهه يسجد ويخضع وبيده يسأل ويرغب ويرهب ويتبتّل وبرأسه يستقبله في ركوعه وسجوده، وبرجليه يقوم ويقعد

"The servant has been commanded to perform the wuḍū so as to be pure when standing before the All-Powerful and supplicating, and by obeying Him, to be purged from filth and impurity, beside his removing laziness, expelling sleep and purifying the heart to stand in the Presence of the All-Powerful. Confining it (the wuḍū) only to the face, the two hands, the head and the two feet, was because when the servant stands before the All-Powerful, the parts which are exposed are those which are ordered to be washed in the wuḍū: as with his face he performs the sujūd (prostration), with his hands he requests, desires, dreads and supplicates, with his head he inclines to Him in his rukūʿ (bowing down) and his sujūd, and with his legs he stands and sits."[3]

13- Contemplate on the philosophy of wudu at each step and perform the recommended acts

The spiritual journey towards Allah (swt) at the time of prayer begins at the time of wuḍū. This means that as you begin your wuḍū, your heart and mind must be present as you go through each step of washing. Thereafter, this conscious presence can be carried forward into prayer. The following are descriptions of the philosophy of each step of wuḍū and some recommended acts that can be practised:

- If possible, face the qiblah as you perform your wuḍū.

- Begin with *"Bi 'ismi Allāh al-Raḥmān al-Raḥīm."*

- Gargle with water prior to wuḍū as this will purify your mouth from any lies, backbiting and other forbidden acts you may have said.

- Rinse your nose with water as this removes any arrogance and pride within you.

- As you wash your face, remember the Day of Resurrection when there will be faces that are illuminated with satisfaction and happiness and faces that are darkened with dissatisfaction and sadness.

- As you wash your right hand, ask Allah (swt) to make you amongst the people of the right (righteous people), and as you wash your left hand, ask Him to keep you away from the people of the left (sinful people).

- As you wipe your head, ask Allah to clear your mind from any evil thoughts and ask Him to help you clear your mind for prayer.

- Finally, as you wipe your feet, ask Allah to make you amongst those who will walk on the Right Path, the path of Muḥammad (saw) and his progeny (as).

It is recommended to recite sūrah al-Qadr (97) during the wuḍū; it is also recommended to recite the following supplications during wuḍū:[4]

Beginning of the wuḍū:

بِسْمِ اللَّهِ وَ بِاللَّهِ وَ الْحَمْدُ لِلَّهِ الَّذِي جَعَلَ الْمَاءَ طَهُوراً وَ لَمْ يَجْعَلْهُ نَجِساً

[I am performing this wuḍū] in the name of Allah and for the sake of Allah; all praise be to Allah who made the water pure and did not make it impure.

While washing the hands twice:

اللَّهُمَّ اجْعَلْنِي مِنْ التَّوَّابِينَ، وَاجْعَلْنِي مِنْ الْمُتَطَهِّرِينَ

O Allah, place me among those who ask for forgiveness and among those who are pure.

While gargling:

اللَّهُمَّ لَقِّنِّي حُجَّتِي يَوْمَ أَلْقَاكَ وَ أَطْلِقْ لِسَانِي بِذِكْرِكَ وَ شُكْرِكَ

O Allah, teach me the correct answer for the day I shall meet You and open my tongue for Your praise.

While rinsing the nose:

اللَّهُمَّ لَا تُحَرِّمْ عَلَيَّ رِيحَ الْجَنَّةِ وَ اجْعَلْنِي مِمَّنْ يَشَمُّ رِيحَهَا وَ رَوْحَهَا وَ طِيبَهَا

Do not deprive me of the scent of Paradise, and place me among those who will inhale its fragrance, its essence and perfume.

While washing the face:

اللَّهُمَّ بَيِّضْ وَجْهِي يَوْمَ تَسْوَدُّ فِيهِ الْوُجُوهُ وَ لَا تُسَوِّدْ وَجْهِي يَوْمَ تَبْيَضُّ فِيهِ الْوُجُوهُ

O Allah! Brighten my face on the day that You will disgrace the faces; and do not disgrace my face on the day that You will brighten the faces.

While washing the right forearm:

اللَّهُمَّ أَعْطِنِي كِتَابِي بِيَمِينِي وَ الْخُلْدَ فِي الْجِنَانِ بِيَسَارِي وَ حَاسِبْنِي حِسَاباً يَسِيراً

O Allah! Place my scroll of deeds in my right hand and (the certificate of) permanency in the Paradise on my left; and do the reckoning of my account leniently.

While washing the left forearm:

اللَّهُمَّ لَا تُعْطِنِي كِتَابِي بِيَسَارِي وَ لَا تَجْعَلْهَا مَغْلُولَةً إِلَى عُنُقِي وَ أَعُوذُ بِكَ رَبِّي مِنْ مُقَطَّعَاتِ النِّيرَانِ

O Allah! Do not place my scroll of deeds in my left hand; and do not make it strap around my neck. And I seek refuge with You from the fierce fire.

While wiping the head:

اللَّهُمَّ غَشِّنِي بِرَحْمَتِكَ وَ بَرَكَاتِكَ وَ عَفْوِكَ

O Allah! Cover me with Your mercy, Your blessings and Your pardon.

While wiping the feet:

اللَّهُمَّ ثَبِّتْنِي عَلَى الصِّرَاطِ يَوْمَ تَزِلُّ فِيهِ الْأَقْدَامُ وَ اجْعَلْ سَعْيِي فِيمَا يُرْضِيكَ عَنِّي يَا ذَا الْجَلَالِ وَ الْإِكْرَامِ

O Allah, keep me steadfast on my path on the day when the feet shall slip; and make my efforts (in the way) that will please You - O Master of power and honour.

14- Avoid excessive doubting in wudu

Some are plagued by continuous doubts causing them to repeat their wuḍū several times; this inevitably interrupts the spiritual significance of the action and steers focus away from the benefits of wuḍū in enabling mental preparation for prayer. The scholars have given an ideal solution to such obsessions: simply avoid doubt and move on. It is narrated from Imām al-Ṣādiq (as) that these doubts are from Shayṭān:

عن عبد الله بن سنان قال: ذكرت لأبي عبدالله (عليه السلام) رجلاً مبتلى بالوضوء والصلاة وقلت : هو رجل عاقل ، فقال أبو عبدالله (عليه السلام) : وأي عقل له وهو يطيع الشيطان ، فقلت له : وكيف يطيع الشيطان ؟ فقال (عليه السلام) : سله هذا الذي يأتيه من أي شيء هو فإنه يقول لك من عمل الشيطان

"Abd Allah ibn Sinān said: 'I mentioned before Imām al-Ṣādiq (as) about a man who was afflicted with performing wuḍū and ṣalāt repetitively, and described him to be a man of reason.' The Imām said: 'What reason has he in obeying Shayṭān?' I asked him: 'How is it that he is obeying Shayṭān?' He said: 'If you ask him wherefrom his hesitation comes to him, he will tell you himself it is the work of Shayṭān.'"[5]

Attempt to concentrate on the benefits of wuḍū in addition to the strict validity of it. The jurisprudence of wuḍū is, of course, essential, but it should not dominate one's mind to the extent that one cannot think of anything else. Allah (swt) says, after He describes how to perform the wuḍū:

مَا يُرِيدُ اللَّهُ لِيَجْعَلَ عَلَيْكُمْ مِنْ حَرَجٍ وَلَٰكِنْ يُرِيدُ لِيُطَهِّرَكُمْ وَلِيُتِمَّ نِعْمَتَهُ عَلَيْكُمْ لَعَلَّكُمْ تَشْكُرُونَ

Allah does not desire to put you to hardship, but He desires to purify you, and to complete His blessing upon you so that you may give thanks. (5:6)

15- Give importance to cleanliness and tidiness

Islam greatly emphasises cleanliness, which has both spiritual and physical benefits. Spiritually, it cleanses the soul and thus makes it difficult for Shayṭān to inculcate intrusive thoughts into the mind during prayer. Physically, cleanliness gives you the comfort and relaxation needed prior to prayer. It is important to note here that there is a distinction between cleanliness (naẓāfah) and purity (ṭahārah) as the latter is obligatory for the acceptance of the prayer.

Some practical suggestions that apply prior to prayer include:

a. If time permits, take a shower to clean yourself so you face Allah (swt) with a clean body. Enter the shower with an intention to purify yourself from any sins before you meet Allah (swt). (Note: the shower here does not compensate for the wuḍū).

b. Some 'aḥādīth emphasise the use of the siwāk, as narrated by Prophet Muḥammad (saw):

لولا أن أشق على أمتي لأمرتهم بالسواك مع كل صلاة

"If it was not for the difficulty that it may cause to my 'ummah, I would have ordered them to use the 'siwāk' during every prayer."[6]

The siwāk helps to refresh the breath and give it a pleasant smell. Alternatively one can use a toothbrush.

c. Make the place of worship clean and tidy. Some report that an untidy place of worship will be a major distracting factor in their concentration during prayer. The believer should therefore make sure that the place they plan to pray is tidy. This will not only relax and quieten the mind, but will also ensure less distraction during prayer.

16- Wear appropriate clothing

It is narrated from Imām ʿAlī (as) that he said:

إن الانسان إذا كان في الصلاة فإن جسده وثيابه وكل شيء حوله يسبح

"When man is praying, his body, his clothes and everything else surrounding him glorifies [Allah]."[7]

There are a few points to consider when choosing the right clothes to wear that can help us concentrate during prayer:

a. The clothes we wear should be comfortable.

b. As well as wearing ritually pure clothes, which is obligatory for prayer, a believer should face Allah (swt) with clean clothes that do not have an unpleasant odour that might detract his/her focus away. It is narrated that Imām ʿAlī (as) said:

النظيف من الثياب يذهب الهم والحزن، وهو طهور للصلاة

"Clothes express beauty. Clean clothes remove sorrow and unhappiness and are necessary for prayer."[8]

c. Our clothes should not contain things that can act as distractions to us or fellow believers whilst praying. They should preferably be plain and white.

d. The clothes should not be excessively luxurious so one does not appear arrogant in front of Allah (swt).

e. It is also mustaḥab to wear a khātim ring with ʿaqīq stone while praying.

Al-Shahīd al-Shaykh ʿAli Al-Jabaʿī al-ʿĀmilī (also known as al-Shahīd al-Thāni) has elaborated on the meaning of wearing the appropriate clothing both physically and metaphorically by saying:

> "The best adornment of the believer's garment is precaution and the most blessed garment is belief. As Allah said, *Yet the garment of Godwariness—that is the best.* (7:26)
>
> Outward dress is a blessing from Allah to preserve the modesty of the sons of Adam; it is a mark of honour which Allah has given to the descendants of Adam. He did not give that honour to any other creature; it is given to the believers as a means of carrying out their obligations. Your best garments are those that do not distract you from Allah, those garments, in fact, which bring you closer to His remembrance, and gratitude and obedience to Him. They should not be such as to move you to pride, conceit, pretence, boastfulness or arrogance: those things are the scourge of the faith, and their legacy is hardness of heart.
>
> When you put on your clothes, remember that Allah veils your wrong actions with His mercy. You should clothe your inward part as you clothe your outward part with your garment. Let your inward truth be veiled in awe of Allah, and let your outward truth be veiled in obedience. Take heed of the overflowing favour of Allah, since He created the means to make garments for covering physical immodesty and opened the gates for repentance, regret, and seeking succour, in order to veil the inward parts, and their wrong actions and bad character.
>
> Do not expose anyone's faults when Allah has concealed worse things in yourself. Occupy yourself with your own faults, and overlook matters and situations that do not

concern you. Beware lest you exhaust your life in other people's actions and exchange your irreplaceable endowed wealth with someone else, thereby destroying yourself. Forgetting wrong actions brings about the greatest of Allah's punishments in this world, and is the most ample cause for punishment in the next. So long as the bondsman occupies himself with obeying Allah, with recognizing his own faults and leaving alone whatever might devalue faith in Allah, he is spared ruin and is immersed in the sea of Allah's mercy, attaining the gems and the benefits of wisdom and clarity.

But as long as he forgets his own wrong actions, is ignorant of his own faults, and falls back on his power and strength, he will never be successful."[9]

17- Put on perfume before prayer

It is mustaḥab for the believer to put on perfume, and especially musk before prayer, as it is narrated from Imām ʿAlī (as):

نِعْمَ الطِّيبُ الْمِسْكُ، خَفِيفٌ مَحْمِلُهُ، عَطِرٌ رِيحُهُ

"The best scent is musk; its weight is light while its smell is fragrant."[10]

There are two main reasons for this, firstly as you stand in front of Allah, The Exalted, and embark on this spiritual journey, it is advisable to meet Allah with a beautiful fragrance.

يَا بَنِي آدَمَ خُذُوا زِينَتَكُمْ عِنْدَ كُلِّ مَسْجِدٍ وَكُلُوا وَاشْرَبُوا وَلَا تُسْرِفُوا ۚ إِنَّهُ لَا يُحِبُّ الْمُسْرِفِينَ

O Children of Adam! Put on your adornment on every occasion of prayer, and eat and drink, but do not waste; indeed He does not like the wasteful. (7:31)

This verse advises us to approach the prayer with the adornment of perfume. This is how Allah (swt) wants His servants to meet Him during prayer. Some interpret 'embellishments' as practicing purity of character and spiritual excellence while approaching prayer.

Secondly the pleasant fragrance creates a spiritual environment for the believer and may increase his attention during prayer.

18- Choose a quiet and comfortable place to worship

Location and atmosphere is essential. Attempt to perform the following prior to prayer:

a. Switch off the TV during prayers, even if the TV is switched on for children.

b. If you have children, teach them to be quiet while you are praying and put away their toys. Explain to them why this is important. You may like to encourage them to pray with you, especially if they are older than around seven years old.

c. Switch off/silence (not vibrate) mobile phones.

d. Remove any pictures in front of you that might distract you during prayer.

e. You may like to allocate a special room for prayers, such that an association develops between that room and meeting Allah (swt). This may not appeal to some who prefer alternating the place of prayer for better concentration (see point 83)

19- Plan which surah to recite in advance

In the first and second units of prayer, the believer has the option of choosing which sūrah to recite from the Holy Qur'ān after sūrah al-Fātiḥah. Usually a short sūrah is chosen. It is recommended to decide this before commencing the prayer. The reasons for this include:

a. Practicing the recitation of a particular sūrah ensures the correct pronunciation and tajwīd rules are applied during the prayer.

b. It can prove as a viable indicator for reflection after prayer for how well we have concentrated during prayer.

c. Understanding and contemplating the meanings of the 'āyāt in the sūrah help us focus on the meanings of the 'āyāt while reciting during prayer. Allah (swt) says in the Holy Qur'ān:

كِتَابٌ أَنْزَلْنَاهُ إِلَيْكَ مُبَارَكٌ لِيَدَّبَّرُوا آيَاتِهِ وَلِيَتَذَكَّرَ أُولُو الْأَلْبَابِ

[It is] a blessed Book that We have sent down to you, so that they may contemplate its signs, and that those who possess intellect may take admonition. (38:29)

أَفَلَا يَتَدَبَّرُونَ الْقُرْآنَ أَمْ عَلَىٰ قُلُوبٍ أَقْفَالُهَا

Do they not contemplate the Qur'ān, or are there locks on the hearts? (47:24)

Would you want to recite the verses while your heart is locked? To open the lock, attempt to read the exegesis of the verses you plan to recite during prayer and ponder over their deep meanings so you may remember the meanings during recitation in prayer. If you are short of time, you may want to read and contemplate the summary of the meanings of the sūrah (but of course it is highly advisable to read the exegesis of every verse). For instance, if you plan to recite sūrah al-Shams (91), contemplate that Allah (swt) swears by eleven of His creations to emphasise that the only way one can achieve happiness and satisfaction is through the purification of the heart. Thus concentration while reciting the sūrah can certainly be achieved with the contemplation on the eleven creations of Allah (swt) and the overall meaning of this sūrah.

20-Contemplate on the creation of Allah (swt)

To be spiritually 'charged' for prayer, try to remind yourself of Allah's presence and creation. This can be done by contemplating on the wonders of Allah's creation. Allah (swt) says in the Holy Qur'ān:

إِنَّ فِي خَلْقِ السَّمَاوَاتِ وَالْأَرْضِ وَاخْتِلَافِ اللَّيْلِ وَالنَّهَارِ لَآيَاتٍ لِأُولِي الْأَلْبَابِ

الَّذِينَ يَذْكُرُونَ اللَّهَ قِيَامًا وَقُعُودًا وَعَلَىٰ جُنُوبِهِمْ وَيَتَفَكَّرُونَ فِي خَلْقِ

السَّمَاوَاتِ وَالْأَرْضِ رَبَّنَا مَا خَلَقْتَ هَٰذَا بَاطِلًا سُبْحَانَكَ فَقِنَا عَذَابَ النَّارِ

Indeed in the creation of the heavens and the earth and the alternation of night and day, there are signs for those who possess intellects. Those who remember Allah standing, sitting, and lying on their sides, and reflect on the creation of the heavens and the earth [and say], 'Our Lord, You have not created this in vain! Immaculate are You! Save us from the punishment of the Fire.' (3:190-191)

It is not shameful for a believer to acknowledge that their belief in Allah is weak and in need of strengthening. As believers, we also need to continuously remind ourselves of the bounties and wonderful gifts that Allah has given us so we strengthen our hearts and thus be confident of His presence. As we stand before Allah (swt) in preparation for prayer, we must ponder over the all the physiological systems within our bodies, operating beautifully to keep us alive, beginning from the circulation of blood, heartbeats, the immune system, the nervous system and respiration to gene function. Furthermore, we should contemplate on what is around us, from the marvels of the cosmos, the animal world and the seas to the microbial world of bacteria and viruses. We have only to look up at the sky and ponder over the miraculous precision of the planets and the sun, the Milky Way and the universe. As we contemplate on these signs, we say:

رَبَّنَا مَا خَلَقْتَ هَٰذَا بَاطِلًا سُبْحَانَكَ فَقِنَا عَذَابَ النَّارِ

'Our Lord, You have not created this in vain! Immaculate are You! Save us from the punishment of the Fire.' (3:191)

Moreover, you may wish to pray outdoors (for example, your garden) and contemplate on the creation of Allah prior to prayer. If this is not possible, you may take a short walk and contemplate the beautiful creation of the Almighty.

21- Relax your mind

The mind must be in a state of comfort to achieve true submission to Allah. If you are tired, have just had an argument with someone, or had a stressful day at work, you should try to relax and focus on the journey ahead. Different people use different techniques to relax, but the most common is to sit down for a few minutes and close your eyes, take a few deep breaths, clear your head and try to focus only on Allah (swt). Of course, this is far easier said than done, but certainly becomes easier with practice. It is reported that great scholars, such as the martyr Muḥammad Bāqir al-Sadr, used to sit for as long as necessary prior to prayer to clear their mind and attempt to be in the vicinity of Allah (swt).

For further suggestions on the techniques used to relax your mind, refer to Chapter Seven of this book and the wider literature on meditation and relaxation techniques.

22- Treat this prayer as if it is your last

Allah (swt) says in the Holy Qur'ān, in sūrah Luqmān:

إِنَّ اللَّهَ عِنْدَهُ عِلْمُ السَّاعَةِ وَيُنَزِّلُ الْغَيْثَ وَيَعْلَمُ مَا فِي الْأَرْحَامِ ۖ وَمَا تَدْرِي نَفْسٌ مَاذَا تَكْسِبُ غَدًا ۖ وَمَا تَدْرِي نَفْسٌ بِأَيِّ أَرْضٍ تَمُوتُ ۚ إِنَّ اللَّهَ عَلِيمٌ خَبِيرٌ

Indeed the knowledge of the Hour is with Allah. He sends down the rain, and He knows what is in the wombs. No soul knows what it will earn tomorrow, and no soul knows in what land it will die. Indeed Allah is all-Knowing, all-Aware. (31:34)

No one knows when or where they will depart from this life. Try to imagine how you would pray your last prayer, with the upmost submission and concentration. Imām al-Ṣādiq (as) emphasised this in the following narration:

يا عبد الله إذا صليت صلاة فريضة فصلها لوقتها صلاة مودع يخاف أن لا يعود إليها، ثم اصرف ببصرك إلى موضع سجودك، فلو تعلم من عن يمينك وعن شمالك لأحسنت صلاتك، واعلم أنك بين يدي من يراك ولا تراه

"O Servant of Allah! When you offer prayer, pray like someone who bids farewell and fears that he will never return (i.e. pray in such a manner as if it were the last prayer of your life). Then fix your gaze on the point of your prostration. If you know that there is someone on your left or right, you take more care in offering your prayer; then know that you stand in front of Someone Who sees you even though you don't see Him."[11]

23- Write down your thoughts and worries

Research suggests that one of the best ways to improve concentration is to write down your thoughts. This unleashes any worldly thoughts that occupy the mind. It will also identify any obstructive thoughts so that you can address them later.

Moreover, if you have a particular problem that is causing your mind to be restless, you might want to map out your thoughts prior to prayer using a problem-solution mind map. The idea is to write down 'problem' at the top of a blank piece of paper and map out every single detail and nature of the problem. As you complete this, write down 'solution' on the same paper and map out all possible solutions to this problem. This exercise will calm you down and make the solutions to the problem clear.

Other forms of mental distractions are worries. Dr Sarfraz Jeraj, a psychologist, writes for this book:

> "Theories of worry and rumination include positive beliefs (conscious or unconscious) about worry. For example, someone might have a pressing issue on their mind and therefore will worry about finding a solution to this issue or worry to ensure he does not forget. Worries can therefore become very distracting in prayer. It may be useful to mentally 'park' these worries. This assures us that we can stop worrying about something temporarily without having the anxiety that it will be forgotten. This can be done by recording the worry or task we need to do on a post-it-note to come back to it later on after completing the prayer. Therefore, if you have a worry and are approaching prayer, write it down prior to approaching prayer so the worry does not distract you during the prayer."

24- Comprehend the philosophy of facing Makkah

When facing the qiblah, turn away from all other directions and face the sanctuary of Allah (swt). Turn your heart away from all matters apart from Allah. Make your heart turn towards one of the most ancient bases of monotheism, the centre of tawḥīd and Prophethood. Remember the history of Makkah and the time when the Father of the Prophets, Prophet Ibrāhīm (as) was ordered to build the Ka'bah and settle his family in this barren land for one main mission: prayer.

رَبَّنَا إِنِّي أَسْكَنْتُ مِنْ ذُرِّيَّتِي بِوَادٍ غَيْرِ ذِي زَرْعٍ عِنْدَ بَيْتِكَ الْمُحَرَّمِ رَبَّنَا لِيُقِيمُوا الصَّلَاةَ فَاجْعَلْ أَفْئِدَةً مِنَ النَّاسِ تَهْوِي إِلَيْهِمْ وَارْزُقْهُمْ مِنَ الثَّمَرَاتِ لَعَلَّهُمْ يَشْكُرُونَ

Lord! I have settled part of my descendants in a barren valley, by Your sacred House, our Lord, that they may maintain the prayer. So make the hearts of a part of the people fond of them, and provide them with fruits, so that they may give thanks. (14:37)

Ask Allah (swt) to make your heart yearn towards the Ka'bah and purify your soul for prayer as Allah ordered Prophet Ibrāhīm (as) to purify this land and the people who make tawāf, pray, bow and prostrate:

وَإِذْ بَوَّأْنَا لِإِبْرَاهِيمَ مَكَانَ الْبَيْتِ أَنْ لَا تُشْرِكْ بِي شَيْئًا وَطَهِّرْ بَيْتِيَ لِلطَّائِفِينَ وَالْقَائِمِينَ وَالرُّكَّعِ السُّجُودِ

When We settled for Abraham the site of the House [saying], Do not ascribe any partners to Me, and purify My House for those who go around it, and those who stand [in it for prayer], and those who bow and prostrate. (22:26)

And finally, as you face the qiblah, think about the fact that millions of people from different parts of the world are praying towards the Ka'bah and feel the spiritual energy emanating from all the believers uniting under the banner of tawḥīd and prayer.

25- Find Allah in your heart and stand in front of Him with piety

As you stand and face the qiblah, empty your heart of all the preoccupations that might distract you from concentrating in your prayer and fill it with the love of Allah (swt). Take a few minutes to search for Him. If you are sincere in your quest, you will find Him because He is nearer to us than our jugular vein (50:16). Once you find Him, stand in front of Him with piety and fear and recognise the beauty of the Lord through your heart. To help you do this and to soften the heart, it helps to arrive early for this journey towards Allah, and spend time reading the Holy Qur'ān or contemplating the existence and creation of Allah (swt). Spend at least five minutes reading and comprehending the Holy Qur'ān before prayer. This will make you dwell in the vicinity of Allah (swt) and away from the whispers of the Shayṭān.

Spending time reading and pondering over the words of the Holy Qur'ān, without doubt, significantly aids concentration and connection to Allah (swt) during prayer. Reading the words of Allah (swt) and His communication with us makes the heart strong, illuminated and ready to meet the Lord.

Furthermore, it is important to contemplate the greatness of the words by sensing the greatness of the Author. As you read the verses, feel the presence of the Throne and His Dominion in your heart and attempt to understand the inner meanings of the verses. Become adorned with the characteristics of every verse. For example, if mercy and the promise of forgiveness are mentioned, become joyful and happy, and if anger and punishment are mentioned, become overtaken with fear. In this way, your mind and soul will react to the characteristics of the verses and you will be in complete contemplation of the Holy Qur'ān. This will undoubtedly prepare you for the journey ahead. Allah (swt) says:

أَفَلَا يَتَدَبَّرُونَ الْقُرْآنَ ۚ وَلَوْ كَانَ مِنْ عِنْدِ غَيْرِ اللَّهِ لَوَجَدُوا فِيهِ اخْتِلَافًا كَثِيرًا

Do they not ponder on the Qur'ān? And if it were from any other than Allah, they would have found in it many a discrepancy. (4:82)

26- Identify factors that distract you in prayer and eliminate them

To eliminate the obstructive thoughts in your head before prayer, it is best to identify the factors that distract you beforehand, and then try to eliminate them. For example, if you are distracted by your children during prayer, you may want to delay your prayer slightly until you find the opportunity to pray in silence. Try your utmost but know that if you cannot, then Allah (swt) does not expect more than what you are capable of as He mentions in sūrah al-Najm.

وَأَنْ لَيْسَ لِلْإِنْسَانِ إِلَّا مَا سَعَىٰ

وَأَنَّ سَعْيَهُ سَوْفَ يُرَىٰ

And that nothing belongs to man except what he strives for, and that he will soon be shown his endeavour. (53:39-40)

27- Complete unfinished tasks

If an unfinished task will affect your concentration during prayer, you could complete the task before approaching prayer. However, if the unfinished task is predicted to take a long time to complete then the prayer must be performed first. For example, if you began cooking before the prayer time and the call for prayer was announced, the you would have to assess whether your concentration would be worsened by thinking about the cooking or not. You should be able to judge and decide appropriately in each circumstance.

28- Recite the 'adhan (call for prayer)

When the time of prayer is established, it is the time for meeting and recognising Allah (swt). To announce this spiritual occasion, Allah (swt) has ordained the 'adhān.

Allah (swt) says in sūrah al-Mā'idah:

وَإِذَا نَادَيْتُمْ إِلَى الصَّلَاةِ اتَّخَذُوهَا هُزُوًا وَلَعِبًا ۚ ذَٰلِكَ بِأَنَّهُمْ قَوْمٌ لَا يَعْقِلُونَ

And when you call to prayer they make it a mockery and a joke; this is because they are a people who do not understand. (5:58)

Calling for prayer, or 'adhān, is a greatly emphasised practice of preparing for prayer. We begin and end with Allah, as we recite Allah is Greater, acknowledge His Oneness and His Prophet, hasten to prayer, happiness and the best acts (i.e. prayer) and affirm that there is no god but Allah. If recited sincerely, it will no doubt set the scene for the spiritual journey to Allah (swt) during prayer. It is narrated that the Prophet Muḥammad (saw) said:

المؤذنون أطول النّاس أعناقاً يوم القيامة

"Those who call for Allah (mu'adhdhin) will have the longest necks (i.e. will be the most exalted) on the Day of Judgment."[12]

There is a tendency amongst the believers however to ignore the 'adhān and merely recite the 'iqāmah prior to prayer. This is due to a lack of appreciation of the benefits of the 'adhān, which is described in this narration from Imām al-Ṣādiq (as):

من أذن وأقام صلى وراءه صفان من الملائكة، وإن أقام بغير أذان صلى عن يمينه واحد، وعن شماله واحد، ثم قال: اغتنم الصفين

"Whoever recites the adhan and the iqamah, two rows of angels will perform the prayer behind him; but if he recites the iqamah without the adhan, one will pray on his right and one on his left and then (the angel) says: the two rows have been done (referring to the two rows comprising of only two people)"[13]

Some points to ponder on:

a. When you hear the call for prayer imagine the call for resurrection:

وَاسْتَمِعْ يَوْمَ يُنَادِ الْمُنَادِ مِنْ مَكَانٍ قَرِيبٍ

And be on the alert for the day; when the caller calls from a close quarter. (50:41)

b. As you hear the 'adhān and remember Allah (swt), let happiness enter your heart, imagine awaiting the good news as your fate is announced on the Day of Judgment 'inshā Allāh.

c. When you hear the three calls beginning with the word 'ḥayyah' (make haste) recited in the 'adhān, prepare yourself to make haste towards prayer, towards success and towards the best and most rewarding task and recite:

لا حول ولا قوة الا بالله العلي العظي

"There is no might or power except in Allah, the Mighty, the Wise."[14]

29- Perform sujud between 'adhan and 'iqamah

It is narrated from Imām 'Alī (as) that he said:

من سجد بين الأذان والاقامة وقال:(رب سجدت لك خاضعا خاشعا ذليلا)
يقول لله تعالى: ملائكتي! وعزتي وجلالي لأجعلن محبته في قلوب عبادي
المؤمنين، وهيبته في قلوب المنافقين

"Anyone who performs prostration between the 'adhān and 'iqāmah and thus says while in prostration, "I prostrate before You humbly, submissively and meekly," Allah (swt) will say: "I swear by my Angels, Honour and Glory, I will place love for him in the hearts of the believers and fear of him in the hearts of the hypocrites [munāfiqīn]."[15]

It is understandable that with our busy lives, we find it difficult to spend much time in prostration before prayer, but spending around a minute prior to prayer in the state of prostration, praising Allah (swt) for His gifts to us, repenting to Him for our sins and asking Allah (swt) for help, can greatly improve concentration and submissiveness during prayer. This brief action, if done with sincerity, can no doubt remove arrogance from our hearts and set us in good stead for our journey to Allah (swt).

30- Recite the 'iqamah

In addition to the 'adhān, reciting the 'iqāmah is also emphasised prior to prayer in order to prepare the believer to reach proximity to Allah (swt) during prayer. 'Adhān is the call to prayer and the 'iqāmah is the opening of the prayer; a shortened form of the 'adhān. 'Iqāmah is the final check to see if our heart is present. When you recite *'Allāhu 'Akbar*, it is the final opportunity before prayer to remove any hatred, anger and arrogance from the heart and to hasten towards the best act. When you recite *'Surely the prayers have been established'*, it is also the time to stand and reach to Allah (swt). And finally, when you recite *'There is no god but Allah'* it is the final check to see if your heart has gained contentment, as described in *Ma'ānī al-Akhbār*:

> "For Allah is the clear proof against the people through His Messenger(s), His message, His explanation and His call. And He is Majestic than for anybody to possess any argument against Him. So whoever answers Him, for him is light and honour. And one who denies Him, then indeed Allah is needless of the universe and He is the quickest in accounting."[16]

31- Recite du'a after 'iqamah

It is recommended to recite a du'ā' or verses of the Qur'ān after the 'iqāmah and before takbīrat al-'iḥrām:

Qur'ānic Du'ā' After 'Iqāmah

إِنِّي وَجَّهْتُ وَجْهِيَ لِلَّذِي فَطَرَ السَّمَاوَاتِ وَالأَرْضَ حَنِيفًا وَمَا أَنَاْ مِنَ الْمُشْرِكِينَ

Indeed I have turned my face toward Him who originated the heavens and the earth, as a ḥanīf, and I am not one of the polytheists.'(6:79)

قُلْ إِنَّ صَلاَتِي وَنُسُكِي وَمَحْيَايَ وَمَمَاتِي لِلّهِ رَبِّ الْعَالَمِينَ

Say, 'Indeed my prayer and my worship, my life and my death are for the sake of Allah, the Lord of all the worlds.' (6:162)

32-Recite a du'a before takbirat al-'ihram

Try to feel the words and their meanings penetrate your heart as you stand in supplication before the Almighty.[17]

Duʿāʾ before Takbīr

يا محسن قد أتاك المسيء وقد أمرت المحسن أن يتجاوز عن المسيء أنت المحسن وأنا المسيء بحق محمد وآل محمد صل على محمد وآل محمد وتجاوز عن قبيح ما تعلم مني

O Lord who is Beneficent! This sinful has come before You and You have ordered the beneficent to show indulgence to the sinners. You are Beneficent, and I am a sinner. Bestow Your blessings on Muḥammad and his progeny, and pardon my evil acts of which You are aware.

اللهم إليك توجهت ومرضاتك ابتغيت وبك آمنت وعليك توكلت ، صل على محمد وآل محمد وافتح قلبي لذكرك وثبتني على دينك ولا تزغ قلبي بعد إذ هديتني وهب لي من لدنك رحمة إنك أنت الوهاب

O Lord, I have turned to You and Your pleasure I seek, and in You I have faith, and in You I rely, send salutations to Muḥammad and his family, and open my heart to continuous remembrance of You, and fix me on Your path, do not cause my heart to deviate (from guidance) after You have guided me, and grant me mercy from Yourself; verily You are the one who grants.

اللهم رب هذه الدعوة التامة والصلاة القائمة بلغ محمدا الدرجة والوسيلة والفضل والفضيلة بالله أستفتح وبالله أستنجح وبمحمد رسول الله أتوجه اللهم صل على محمد وآل محمد واجعلنى بهم عندك وجيها في الدنيا والاخرة ومن المقربين

O Allah! Lord of this perfect call and the established prayer; give Muḥammad the status of mediation and superiority. I begin with Allah and with Allah I succeed and with Muḥammad (saw) I turn my face (towards Allah). O Allah, send salutations to Muḥammad and his family, and make me an honourable person in this world and in the Herefter and amongst the people who are close.

33- Imagine you are standing in front of Allah on the Day of Judgment

As you are about to raise your hands for takbīrat al-'iḥrām, imagine standing in front of the Almighty on the Day of Judgment, waiting for your verdict. Remind yourself that He is the Majesty, the Almighty, the exceedingly Compassionate and Merciful, the Knowing, the King, the Owner, the Divine, the Peace, the Provider, the Exalter and the All-Hearing and the All-Seeing. He is the One who created us, the One who takes life from us and the One that will judge us. Such thoughts, entertained sincerely, should surely be sufficient to fill the heart of the believer with awe.

Conclusion

We should approach the prayer with motivation, a strong heart determined to get closer to Allah (swt) and a continual remembrance that He is aware of our efforts. This attitude will offer us the best opportunity for a successful prayer.

It may be the case that we do not have time to recite the numerous supplications quoted in this chapter. What is important is that the personal conversation with the Almighty begins *before* the prayer. Even if we do not recite the specific du'ā' in Arabic, we should try to speak to Allah (swt) in our own language, sincerely at every step of the preparation, from the wuḍū to the time we stand on our prayer mat.

However, the believer must beware that Shayṭān will cruise around him and enter through any loophole to divert his attention away from the Almighty. Allah (swt) describes the pious as those who notice when the Shayṭān is distracting them and respond by remembering Allah:

إِنَّ الَّذِينَ اتَّقَوْا إِذَا مَسَّهُمْ طَائِفٌ مِنَ الشَّيْطَانِ تَذَكَّرُوا فَإِذَا هُمْ مُبْصِرُونَ

When those who are Godwary are touched by a visitation of Satan, they remember [Allah] and, behold, they perceive. (7:201)

Battling Shayṭān is indeed a jihād, especially at the prayer time. If Shayṭān enters your heart while preparing for prayer, do not give up and give in to him; you must battle against Shayṭān right to the last word in the prayer as he aims to distract you in every possible way so you do not concentrate at all in your prayer. Being aware of his attempts is the first step to shunning him away and hastening towards prayer.

Endnotes

1. al-Kulaynī, *al-Kāfī*, vol. 6, p. 269.
2. Refer to Khomeini, *'Ādāb al-Ṣalāt*: The Disciplines of the Prayer, Discourse 2, Chapters 3, 4 and 5.
3. al-Ṣadūq, *'Uyūn Akhbār al-Riḍā*, vol. 2, p. 104.
4. This supplication has been included as it provides many spiritual lessons of wuḍū that the believer can comprehend for concentration in wuḍū and prayer. This du'ā' can be found online at: [http://www.duas.org/wadhu.htm] 18/03/2014.
5. al-Kulaynī, *al-Kāfī*, vol. 1, p. 12.
6. al-Kulaynī, *al-Kāfī*, vol. 3, p. 22.
7. al-Ṣadūq, *'Ilāl al-Sharāyi'*, vol. 2, p. 336.
8. al-Kulaynī, *al-Kāfī*, vol. 2, p. 203.
9. al-Shahīd al-Thānī, *Rasā'il al-Shahīd al-Thānī*, p. 117.
10. al-Sharīf al-Raḍī, Nahj al-Balāghah, Sayings. 407.
11. al-Ṣadūq, *Thawāb al-'A'māl*, p. 35.
12. al-Ṣadūq, *'Uyūn Akhbār al-Riḍā,* vol. 2, p. 61.
13. al-Ṣadūq, *Man Lā Yaḥḍuruh al-Faqīh*, vol. 1, p. 28.
14. Dastghayb, *Salāt Khāshi'īn*, p. 47.
15. Ibn Ṭāwūs, *Falāḥ al-Sā'īl*, p. 152.
16. al-Ṣadūq, *Ma'ānī al-'Akhbār* p. 41.
17. These du'ā' have been taken from Yazdi, M. Comments by al-Sistānī. A. *al-Urwatul Withqa*. Part Two, p. 117-118.

Chapter 4: The Prayer

At this stage, the believer is ready to embark on this spiritual journey to the love and pleasure of Allah (swt). He will be filled with awe and fear of his Lord, and submits completely with his mind and heart to the One and Only Omnipotent Creator. The following are some ideas that might help the believer along this magnificent journey.

In this chapter:

34. Have a sincere nīyyah (intention)
35. Know that your hand movement in takbīrat al-'iḥrām is a symbol of leaving worldly matters
36. Regard all creatures as small in relation to the greatness of Allah
37. Perform multiple takbīr and recite du'ā
38. Seek refuge with Allah from Shayṭān
39. Contemplate the meaning of the Basmalah
40. Appreciate the significance of sūrah al-Fātiḥah
41. Contemplate the exegesis of sūrah al-Fātiḥah
42. Contemplate the exegesis of sūrah al-'Ikhlāṣ
43. Recite 'Al-ḥamdu li 'Allāh Rabbi al-'ālamīn' after sūrah al-Fātiḥah and 'Kadhālika Allāhu Rabbī' after reciting sūrah al-'Ikhlāṣ

44. Supplicate to Allah (swt) as you recite the verses
45. Alternate recitation of the second sūrah
46. Imagine you are writing what you recite
47. Pause after reciting each verse
48. Recite with a beautiful voice
49. Learn new invocations in qunūt
50. Understand the philosophy behind rukū'
51. Perform the recommended acts in the rukū'
52. Alternate the tasbīḥ in the rukū' and sujūd
53. Praise Allah for hearing your glorification
54. Understand the philosophy of sujūd
55. Prolong your sujūd as much as you can
56. Recite du'ā between the two sujūd and during and after sujūd
57. Contemplate on the meaning of the tasbīḥ in the third and/or fourth rak'at
58. Focus on the true meanings of the taslīm
59. Imagine every part of your body will bear witness to the oneness of Allah (swt)
60. Remember the greatness of the Prophet (saw) and his progeny during taslīm
61. Recite the recommended du'ā during the tashahhud and taslīm
62. If you lose concentration, bounce back fast
63. Pray at a measured pace
64. Fix your gaze during prayer
65. Shed some tears during prayer while contemplating non-worldy affairs
66. Avoid continuous doubting and obsessive repetition of verses
67. Face the ground in humility

34- Have a sincere niyyah (intention)

A sincere nīyyah (intention) is the first test of your sincerity in prayer. Having a sincere nīyyah in prayer means praying solely to Allah (swt) and only for His sake. The intention must be to please Him and no-one else, without expecting worldly rewards.

As you affirm your intention (either verbally or in your heart) you should remember it until the end of the prayer. This means that you must be conscious of your intentions throughout the prayer and never allow worldly thoughts to penetrate the soul. Having a sincere, devout intention thus acts as a barrier against misguidance and ensures one is not distracted by secondary motives or concerns.

The nīyyah in prayer must be pure, i.e. must be solely for the pleasure and satisfaction of Allah (swt), otherwise it will be considered void. For example, without realising it, we may slow down our prayer or make it seem that we have more sincerity when someone else is in the room as we pray. Therefore, unintentionally, our nīyyah is no longer for the sake of Allah alone. Once our prayer is not solely for the sake of Allah, the quality of the prayer, as well as our concentration in it, will be affected.

35- Know that your hand movement in takbirat al-'ihram is a symbol of leaving worldly matters

As you lift your hands for takbīrat al-'iḥrām and put them down uttering *'Allāhu 'Akbar* consider your head to be clear from any thoughts other than those relating to Allah (swt). With this hand movement you are symbolically expelling all extraneous thoughts from your head, facilitating full devotion to Allah (swt). The mind and heart should be synchronised and fully devoted to Allah as you are ready to affirm your intention to your Lord.

36- Regard all creatures as small in relation to the greatness of Allah

As we recite *'Allāhu 'Akbar* (Allah is Greater) in takbīrat al-'iḥrām, we affirm our belief that Allah is superior to everyone and everything. We stand with full humility in front of His Majesty without giving any attention to any unworthy creation.

Fayd Kashani in his book *al-Mahajjah al-Bayḍā'* says in this regard:

> "Examine your heart during the ṣalāt. If you tasted the sweetness of the ṣalāt, and if in your soul you felt pleased and happy by it, and your heart enjoyed the supplication to Allah and conversing with Him, know that Allah has approved your takbīr. Otherwise, without feeling pleasure in supplication, and being deprived of tasting the sweetness of worship, you should know that Allah has denied you and dismissed you from His Threshold."[1]

Regarding the meaning of 'Allāhu 'Akbar, it is narrated in the book *Salat (Prayer): The Mode of Divine Proximity and Recognition*:

> "One meaning of 'Allāhu 'Akbar denotes the eternity, everlastingness, knowledge, power, strength, benevolence, endowment, greatness and honour of Allah the Almighty. By saying 'Allāhu 'Akbar, the mu'adhdhin implies, 'Allah is He to whom belong the creation and the command.' He brings everything into creation by His Will. All that the creation possesses is due to Him. Also, its return is unto Him. He is the First, before everything, from eternity. He is the Last, after everything, and is Everlasting. He is Evident, more than anything else, but cannot be comprehended. He is the Hidden, more than anything else, but is without limits. (In other words, His being apparent is more evident than the manifestation of anything else and His concealment is more hidden than anything else)."[2]

37- Perform multiple takbir and recite du'a

It is recommended to perform 3, 5 or 7 takbīr (as in the hand movement during takbīrat al-'iḥrām), also known as 'takbīrat al-'iftitāḥīyyah' or the 'opening takbīr'. According to Sayid Yazdi and as commented by Ayatollah Sistani, you can have the nīyyah of all the takbīrāt as takbīrat al-'iḥrām, but they say its best if one considers the last takbīr to be the takbīrat al-'iḥrām. It is recommended to recite supplications between the takbīr:[3]

Start with three takbīr then recite:

اللهم أنت الملك الحق لا إله إلا أنت سبحانك إني ظلمت نفسي فاغفر لي ذنبي إنه لا يغفر الذنوب إلا أنت

O Allah, You are the Sovereign, none has the right to be worshiped except You. I have wronged my own soul and have acknowledged my sin, so forgive me all my sins for no one forgives sins except You.

Perform two further takbīr then recite

لبيك وسعديك والخير في يديك والشر ليس إليك، والمهدي من هديت، لا ملجأ منك إلا إليك سبحانك وحنانيك وتباركت وتعاليت سبحانك رب البيت

Here I am, in answer to Your call, happy to serve You. All the goodness is in Your hands and evil is not attributed to You.

Perform two final takbīr and begin reciting sūrah al-Fātiḥah

38- Seek refuge with Allah from Shaytan.

Shayṭān has vowed to try his best to divert believers away from the straight path until the Day of Judgment. We should therefore be aware of his attempts and try the following:

a. It is recommended to (quietly) recite with a sincere intention *"A'ūdhū bi Allāh min al-Shayṭān al-rajīm"* which means *"I seek refuge with Allah from the accursed Satan"* before reciting the sūrah of the Holy Qur'ān during prayer.

فَـإِذَا قَـرَأْتَ الْقُـرْآنَ فَاسْـتَعِذْ بِـاللَّهِ مِـنَ الشَّـيْطَانِ الـرَّجِيمِ

إِنَّـهُ لَـيْسَ لَـهُ سُـلْطَانٌ عَـلَى الَّـذِينَ آمَنُـوا وَعَـلَىٰ رَبِّهِـمْ يَتَوَكَّلُـونَ

إِنَّمَا سُلْطَانُهُ عَلَى الَّذِينَ يَتَوَلَّوْنَهُ وَالَّذِينَ هُمْ بِهِ مُشْرِكُونَ

When you recite the Qur'ān, seek the protection of Allah against the outcast Satan. Indeed he does not have any authority over those who have faith and put their trust in their Lord. His authority is only over those who befriend him and those who make him a partner [of Allah]. (16:98-100)

b. Keep away from satanic actions in life. For example, seeking refuge with Allah from Shayṭān in prayer is considered worthless if a person constantly fills their mind with inappropriate thoughts, or constantly looks at what is prohibited. Consider Shayṭān as the 'number one enemy'; if he is present in our souls during our daily lives then it will be difficult to remove him during the prayer. Allah (swt) reminds us:

إِنَّ الشَّيْطَانَ لَكُمْ عَدُوٌّ فَاتَّخِذُوهُ عَدُوًّا ۚ إِنَّمَا يَدْعُو حِزْبَهُ لِيَكُونُوا مِنْ

أَصْحَابِ السَّعِيرِ

Satan is indeed your enemy, so treat him as an enemy. He only invites his confederates so that they may be among the inmates of the Blaze. (35:6)

39- Contemplate the meaning of the Basmalah

As we begin every sūrah with *Bi 'ismi Allāh al-Raḥmān al-Raḥīm* or *In the Name of Allah, the All-Beneficent, the All-Merciful*, it is crucial to comprehend the deep meanings of this verse. Some of these meanings include:

- The Basmalah is the mark of our monotheistic orientation. We must utter *Bi 'ismi Allāh al-Raḥmān al-Raḥīm* before we begin any task so we confirm our sincere belief of tawḥīd.

- Reciting the Basmalah is the deepest form of respect towards Allah (swt) as it teaches us morals and ethics and expresses our love and gratitude towards Him (swt).

- It invokes Allah (swt)'s blessings on a task.

- Beginning with the Name of Allah undoubtedly gives us the strength, the will and the courage to perform the task at hand with complete sincerity and integrity and to the best of our abilities.

- Allah (swt) has thousands of beautiful names and attributes, but He has chosen the name Allah in the Basmalah. The word 'God' in Arabic is 'ilāh, al-'ilāh means 'The God' and al-'ālihah means 'the gods'. Allah therefore is the perfection of the noun; it cannot be made plural or assigned a gender. Allah is the Essence, the One and only who is worthy of love, compassion and worship as He possesses all perfection.

- Imam Khomeini (ra) in his book *'Ādāb al-Ṣalāt* gives an excellent conclusion to the deep meaning of Bi 'ismi Allāh al-Raḥmān al-Raḥīm:

> "the sālik [traveller to Allah] has to inform his heart, when reciting the Basmalah, that all the outward and inward beings and all the visible and invisible worlds, are under the education of the Names of Allah, or rather, they are

> manifest by the manifestation of the Names of Allah, and all his motions and stillness, and all the worlds, are based on the self-existence of the Greatest Name of Allah. So, his praises are for Allah, and his worship, obedience, monotheism and sincerity are all because of the self-existence of the Name of Allah."[4]

- Allah is al-Raḥmān as He is beneficent to all mankind and al-Raḥīm as He is Merciful to the believers, in particular as narrated in *Al-Amthāl fī Tafsīr al-Qur'ān*:

وَاللهُ إِلهُ كُلِّ شَيْءٍ الرَّحْمنُ بِجَمِيعِ خَلْقِهِ، الرَّحِيمُ بِالْمُؤْمِنِينَ خَاصَّةً

"Allah is the Lord of everything, beneficent to all His creation, Merciful to specifically the believers."[5]

- The mercy of Allah (swt) extends to the Day of Judgment, as narrated by the Prophet (saw):

إِنَّ لله عَزَّ وَجَلَّ مائَةَ رَحْمَةٍ، وَإِنَّهُ أَنْزَلَ مِنْهَا واحِدَةً إِلَى الأَرْضِ، فَقَسَّمَهَا بَيْنَ خَلْقِهِ بِهَا يَتَعَاطَفُونَ وَيَتَرَاحَمُونَ، وَأَخَّرَ تِسْعاً وَتِسْعِينَ لِنَفْسِهِ يَرْحَمُ بِهَا عِبَادَهُ يَوْمَ الْقِيَامَةِ

"Allah has divided mercy into one hundred parts; and sent down to earth one part which He has divided between His servants. Through this one part His servants deal with one another with compassion and mercy, and the other ninety-nine for Himself which He provides His servants with on the Day of Judgment."[6]

- By uttering the Basmalah, the heart is purified from all sins by asking Allah for His mercy that encompasses all things.

40- Appreciate the significance of surah al-Fatihah

Imām al-Riḍhā (as) was asked to explain why sūrah al-Fātiḥah must be read in every prayer. It is narrated that he said:

لأنه ليس شئ من القرآن والكلام جمع فيه من جوامع الخير والحكمة ما جمع في سورة الحمد

"This is because you will not find anywhere else in the Qur'ān something that includes a collection of good meanings and wisdom as you do in sūrah al-Ḥamd."[7]

Appreciating the significance of sūrah al-Fātiḥah (or al-Ḥamd or 'Umm al-Kitāb) is vital in facilitating undivided attention in prayer. Sūrah al-Fātiḥah is a very *personal* sūrah. Once it is recited with pure intentions and contemplation, communication with the Almighty can begin without the need for any mediators. The believer must recite the verses with an appreciation of their true significance rather than allowing the recitation to become routine. This is clearly emphasised in this ḥadīth al-qudsī where it is narrated that Allah (swt) said:

قَسَمْتُ الصَّلاةَ بَيْنِي وَبَيْنَ عَبْدِي نِصْفَيْنِ , نِصْفُهَا لِي وَنِصْفُهَا لِعَبْدِي , يَقُولُ الْعَبْدُ : الْحَمْدُ لِلَّهِ رَبِّ الْعَالَمِينَ, يَقُولُ اللَّهُ : حَمِدَنِي عَبْدِي , يَقُولُ الْعَبْدُ : الرَّحْمَنِ الرَّحِيمِ, يَقُولُ اللَّهُ : أَثْنَى عَلَيَّ عَبْدِي , يَقُولُ الْعَبْدُ : مَالِكِ يَوْمِ الدِّينِ, يَقُولُ اللَّهُ : مَجَّدَنِي عَبْدِي , وَهَذِهِ الآيَةُ بَيْنِي وَبَيْنَ عَبْدِي , إِيَّاكَ نَعْبُدُ وَإِيَّاكَ نَسْتَعِينُ, فَهُوَ بَيْنِي وَبَيْنَ عَبْدِي وَلِعَبْدِي مَا سَأَلَ , وَيَقُولُ الْعَبْدُ : اهْدِنَا الصِّرَاطَ الْمُسْتَقِيمَ صِرَاطَ الَّذِينَ أَنْعَمْتَ عَلَيْهِمْ غَيْرِ الْمَغْضُوبِ عَلَيْهِمْ وَلا الضَّالِّينَ فَهُوَ لِعَبْدِي وَلِعَبْدِي مَا سَأَلَ

"I have divided the prayer between Me and My servant, half of it for Me and half of it for My servant. When my servant says: 'In the name of Allah, the Beneficent, the Merciful', Allah says: 'My servant has remembered Me', and when he says: 'All praise is for Allah', Allah says: 'My servant has praised and glorified Me,' and this is the meaning of 'Allah hears from the one who praises Him'. And when he says: 'The Beneficent, the Merciful', Allah says: 'My servant aggrandised Me.' And when he says: 'Master of the Day of Judgment,' Allah says: 'My servant glorified Me.' [In another version: 'My servant has entrusted himself to Me']. And this verse is between Me and my servant. And when he says: 'You alone we worship and You alone we seek help,' Allah says: 'This is between Me and My servant and my servant will get what he asked for.' And when he says: 'Guide us to the straight path, the path of whom You have blessed, not those whom You have sent your wrath nor those who go astray.' Allah says: 'This is my servant and my servant will get what he has asked for.'"[8]

When you begin to recite sūrah al-Fātiḥah, divide the sūrah into two parts. The first part is verses 1 to 4 where you praise and glorify the Almighty (swt). The second part is the remainder of the sūrah where you recite a set of pledges to Allah (swt). Always have this in your mind prior to the recitation. The next point will elaborate further into each verse and their meaning.

41- Contemplate the exegesis of surah al-Fatihah

Understanding the exegesis (or tafsīr) of sūrah al-Fātiḥah allows the deep meaning to penetrate the heart. The following is a brief exegesis of al-Fātiḥah (1:1-7):[9]

بِسْمِ اللَّهِ الرَّحْمَٰنِ الرَّحِيمِ

In the Name of Allah, the Beneficient, the Merciful. (1:1)

- See point 39 for explanation of the Basmalah.

الْحَمْدُ لِلَّهِ رَبِّ الْعَالَمِينَ

All praise belongs to Allah, Lord of all the worlds. (1:2)

- Praising Allah in the form of al-ḥamd is not the same as shukr (thanks) or madḥ (praise), as al-ḥamd is praise and thanks to the extent of worship. As we worship Him and Him alone, this phrase can only be used in association with Allah (swt).

- One may ask, why is Allah praised? The answer lies in the next part of the verse: He is the Lord of all the worlds. Here, 'all the worlds' refer to the sky, the universe and the creatures, from the humans and animals to all other species. The explanation of this is also included in the Holy Qur'ān:

قَالَ فِرْعَوْنُ وَمَا رَبُّ الْعَالَمِينَ قَالَ رَبُّ السَّمَاوَاتِ وَالْأَرْضِ وَمَا بَيْنَهُمَا ۖ إِنْ كُنْتُمْ مُوقِنِينَ

He [Pharaoh] said, 'And what is "the Lord of all the worlds?"' He said, 'The Lord of the heavens and the earth and whatever is between them - should you have conviction.' (26:23-24)

الرَّحْمَٰنِ الرَّحِيمِ

The Beneficient, the Merciful. (1:3)

- See point 39 for explanation and difference between these two attributes of Allah (swt): *al-Raḥmān* and *al-Raḥīm*.

مَالِكِ يَوْمِ الدِّينِ

Master of the Day of Judgment. (1:4)

- Allah is not only the Lord of the universe and everything in it; He is the Owner, Sovereign and Master of the Day of Judgment.

- Man deludes himself into thinking he is the master of his own affairs in this world and tends to neglect the real Master. Here, Allah specifically states He is the Master of the Day of Judgment; no man can claim its mastership. When man is asked on that Day:

لِّمَنِ الْمُلْكُ الْيَوْمَ ۖ لِلَّـهِ الْوَاحِدِ الْقَهَّارِ

'To whom does the sovereignty belong today?' 'To Allah, the One, the All-Paramount!' (40:16)

- Meaning of mālik (master): Man is considered the master of his own body parts and can move them whenever he likes, Allah is the Master of the Day of Judgment and so He decides the fate of all whenever and wherever He likes.

- The link to the previous verse: 'The Beneficent, the Merciful' and this verse: 'Master of the Day of Judgment' is an interesting one. Allah has mentioned two of His greatest attributes and has promised to be beneficent to all mankind. However, in the next verse He reminds mankind that His ultimate justice on the Day of Judgment awaits them.

إِيَّاكَ نَعْبُدُ وَإِيَّاكَ نَسْتَعِينُ

You do we serve and You alone do we beseech for help (1:5)

- After establishing complete obedience and servitude to Allah by praising Him, contemplating Him as the Lord of the worlds, stamping the essence of faith in our hearts with tawḥīd, glorifying Allah with two of His magnificent attributes and remembering the Day of Judgment; the servant is now ready to address his Lord: "*You alone we worship and from You alone we seek help*".

- The verse turns to tawḥīd (unity) of worship and tawḥīd of seeking help in the plural form where it states 'we worship' and 'we turn for help'. This emphasises the importance of congregational prayers and unity in Islam.

- Tawḥīd of worship means that we firmly acknowledge that Allah alone is worthy of worship and tawḥīd of seeking help means that we firmly acknowledge that we should ask help from Allah alone.

- Worship can sometimes be difficult; for example, when concentrating in prayer. In this verse, Allah links worship to seeking help, which encourages us to seek help from Him even when we worship Him.

اهْدِنَا الصِّرَاطَ الْمُسْتَقِيمَ

Guide us on the straight path. (1:6)

- After addressing Allah and pleading for His help, the servant seeks to ask his Lord for the most important request: "*Oh Allah, guide us to the straight path.*"

- Here are three brief explanations of 'the straight path':

• Worshiping Allah:

وَأَنِ اعْبُدُونِي ۚ هَٰذَا صِرَاطٌ مُسْتَقِيمٌ

Worship Me. That is a straight path. (36:61)

• The path of Ibrāhīm (as) and his descendents:

قُلْ إِنَّنِي هَدَانِي رَبِّي إِلَىٰ صِرَاطٍ مُسْتَقِيمٍ دِينًا قِيَمًا مِلَّةَ إِبْـرَاهِيمَ حَنِيفًـا
وَمَا كَانَ مِنَ الْمُشْرِكِينَ

Say, 'Indeed my Lord has guided me to a straight path, the upright religion, the creed of Abraham, a ḥanīf, and he was not one of the polytheists.' (6:161)

- Holding fast to Allah:

وَمَنْ يَعْتَصِمْ بِاللَّهِ فَقَدْ هُدِيَ إِلَىٰ صِرَاطٍ مُسْتَقِيمٍ

And whoever takes recourse in Allah is certainly guided to a straight path. (3:101)

All of the above three meanings share the same core principle: the straight path is the path of true belief in the Divine religion of Allah with its moral and practical aspects. It is the path of righteousness, justice, and faith.

صِرَاطَ الَّذِينَ أَنْعَمْتَ عَلَيْهِمْ غَيْرِ الْمَغْضُوبِ عَلَيْهِمْ وَلَا الضَّالِّينَ

The path of those upon whom You have blessed -such as have not incurred Your wrath, nor are astray. (1:7)

The request from the servant for guidance to the straight path in the previous verse is elaborated in this verse. The servant asks his Lord: "*Keep us on the path of those whom You, O Allah, have blessed; not the path of those who incur Your wrath, nor of those who go astray.*" Who are those whom Allah has blessed? And who are those people who incur His wrath and who go astray?

- As for those whom Allah has blessed, Allah describes them:

وَ مَنْ يُطِعِ ٱلرَّسُولَ فَأُولئِكَ مَعَ ٱلَّذِينَ أَنْعَمَ اللهُ عَلَـيهِم مِـنَ ٱلنَّبِيِّـينَ وَ
ٱلصِّدِّيقِينَ وَ ٱلشُّهَداء وَ ٱلصَّالِحِينَ وَ حَسُنَ أُولٰئِكَ رَفِيقًا

Whoever obeys Allah and the Apostle - they are with those whom Allah has blessed, including the prophets and the truthful, the martyrs[10] and the righteous, and excellent companions are they! (4:69)

An interesting observation in *Al-'Amthāl fī Tafsīr al-Qur'ān*[11] argues that these are four stages that will eventually build the perfect Islamic society: that of the prophets who lived and struggled for the sake of Allah, that of the truthful and sincere individuals who preach for Islam and their words attest to their actions, that of the martyrs who faced injustice and defended the truth for the sake of Allah, and finally the stage of those righteous individuals who spread peace, human rights and respect in a perfect society after it is corrupted with injustice and inhumanity.

When reciting the last verse of al-Fātiḥah, we ask the Almighty in our heart to include us in the ranks of the prophets, the truthful, the martyrs and the righteous.

- There are several interpretations about the identity of those who incur Allah's wrath and who have gone astray. However, the general understanding is that those who have gone astray are the misguided people, and those who incur Allah's wrath are the hypocrites and those who pursue the path of hatred against Allah (swt). The people who incur Allah's wrath are considered to be worse than the people who have gone astray, as the former consciously rebel against Islamic beliefs and principles.

42- Contemplate the exegesis of surah al-'Ikhlas

A brief exegesis of sūrah al-'Ikhlāṣ[12] is given here because of its fundamental and concise guidance to the Oneness of Allah (swt) and that it represents one third of the Qur'ān as narrated by the Holy Prophet (saw):

أيعجز أحدكم أن يقرأ ثلث القرآن في ليلة"؟ قيل: يا رسول الله ومن يطيق ذلك؟ قال:" اقرأوا قل هو الله أحد"

"Is there anyone of you unable to recite one third of the Qur'ān in one night?' One of his listeners asked: 'O Messenger of Allah! Who is able to do that?' The Prophet (saw) said: 'Recite Say: He, Allah, is One!' (sūrah al-'Ikhlāṣ)."[13]

This sūrah represents the purist and sincere monotheistic beliefs, away from polytheism and any association of partners with Allah (swt); this is why the sūrah has been named *'Ikhlāṣ*. It is thus highly recommended to recite this sūrah in the daily prayers as narrated by Imām al-Ṣādiq (as):

من مضى به يوم واحد فصلى فيه بخمس صلوات ولم يقرأ فيها بقل هو الله أحد قيل له: يا عبد الله لست من المصلين

"If a day passes by and the believer does not recite 'Say He Allah is One' (sūrah al-'Ikhlāṣ) in his prayers, they say to him: Oh servant of Allah, you are not amongst those who pray."[14]

The following is a brief exegesis of sūrah al-'Ikhlāṣ (112:1-4):

قُلْ هُوَ اللَّهُ أَحَدٌ

Say: He, Allah, is One (112:1)

- When we recite 'Say He Allah is One' we must comprehend that One does not mean 'one' in a numerical sense (i.e. followed by two and three); rather 'One' means that there is no one like Him and no example of Him.

- He is One as described in the book: *An Enlightening Commentary into the Light of the Holy Qur'ān:*[15] *"He is One with none comparable to Him, without any beginning or end, unlimited by time, space or circumstances. A reality before which all others have no existence. He is the Creator, One, and everything is His creation."*

اللَّهُ الصَّمَدُ

Allah is He on Whom all depend (112:2)

- 'ṣamad' in Arabic is described as 'qaṣd' which means 'seek'. In this context, it means Allah is the master that we seek to satisfy our needs. We are all in need of Him, He is needless and independent of anyone. Other meanings include that He is not material, has no body and does not have bodily features and senses.

لَمْ يَلِدْ وَلَمْ يُولَدْ

He begets not, nor is He begotten (112:3)

- This verse answers the Jews, Christians and the non-believers that Allah does not have a father or son, and that it is impossible for an equal and similar being to be like Him. His relationship with His creation is not like a parent with a child. He is neither in anything nor is anything in Him, as nothing is like Him.

وَلَمْ يَكُنْ لَهُ كُفُوًا أَحَدٌ

And none is like Him (112:4)

- Kufuwan, means equal in position, thus this verse means He has no equal in being, does not have a partner or peer and is the ultimate unique being.

- It is narrated that the Commander of the Faithful (as) said:

لم يلد فيكون مولوداً، ولم يولد فيصير محدوداً... ولا كفء له فيكافئه،

ولا نظير له فيساويه

"He begets not so as to be born, and nor is He begotten and hence limited. He is incomparable to anyone, so no one can be compared to Him, and No one is like Him or equal to Him."[16]

In summary, this sūrah gives a concise and clear explanation of the concept of tawḥīd, one that reveals monotheism and neglects all layers of polytheism. The verses describe Allah by revealing His Oneness as He is One in Essence and Attributes; He is independent and needless of others; He does not reproduce nor is created; He has no equal in being and does not have parents, children or peers.

43- Recite 'Al-hamdullillahi Rabbi Al-a'lamin' after surah al-Fatihah and 'Kadhalika Allahu Rabbi' after reciting surah al-'Ikhlas

After you recite sūrah al-Fātiḥah, take a deep breath and say *Al-ḥamdu li 'Allāh Rabbi Al-'ālamīn*; *Praise be to Allah, Lord of the Words.*[17] This is so you praise Allah (swt) for guiding you to the Right Path and not amongst those who incur Allah's wrath and who have gone astray.

If you decide to recite sūrah al-'Ikhlāṣ in the prayer, it is recommended also to say *Kadhālika Allāhu Rabbī; That is indeed how my Lord is*, after the recitation of the sūrah.[18]

عن عبد العزيز بن المهتدي قال: سألت الرضا عليه السلام عن التوحيد فقال: كل من قرأ قل هو الله أحد وآمن بها فقد عرف التوحيد، قلت : كيف يقرؤها؟ قال: كما يقرؤها الناس وزاد فيه كذلك الله ربي [كذلك الله ربي]

"It is narrated from Abdul Aziz ibn al-Mahtadi that when he asked Imām al-Riḍhā (as) about the Oneness of Allah (tawḥīd), Imām al-Riḍhā replied: Whoever reads 'Say, Allah is One' (sūrah al-

'Ikhlāṣ), believing in it, he will comprehend tawḥīd. Al-Mahtadi then asked: 'How should we read it?' The Imām replied: 'Read it the way people read it,' then he added *'Kadhālika Allāhu Rabbī'* twice."[19]

It is common to recite sūrah al-'Ikhlāṣ after sūrah al-Fātiḥah, as it is recommended practice, yet less attention is given to its meaning. However, if we recite 'Kadhālika Allāhu Rabbī' or 'that is indeed how my Lord is' after reciting the sūrah, the Oneness and glorification of Allah (swt) stated in sūrah al-'Ikhlāṣ is emphasised and this may draw attention back to the prayer.

44- Supplicate to Allah (swt) as you recite the verses.

Try to supplicate to Allah (swt) in your heart from what you read from verses in the sūrah after sūrah al-Ḥamd. So for instance if the contents of the sūrah mention Hellfire then ask Allah (swt) in your heart to distant you from Hellfire on the Day of Judgment and take you to Paradise. If however you recite a verse that mentions the mercy of Allah (swt) then ask for His mercy and forgiveness.

45- Alternate recitation of the second surah

By limiting the recitation of the second sūrah to the same three or four suwar of the Holy Qur'ān, the brain becomes accustomed to repeating these small suwar. Subconsciously our attention will therefore switch to something else. It is in fact makrūh (not recommended) to repeat the same sūrah in the same prayer, except for sūrah al-'Ikhlāṣ. The believer can choose from a range of small chapters to recite, beginning from sūrah al-Ṭāriq (86) to the final sūrah an-Nās. If you have the time and the capability to recite slightly longer chapters then recite from sūrah 78 onwards.[20]

It is recommended to recite certain sūrah from the Qur'ān with certain prayers:[21]

Fajr Prayer: sūrah al-Naba (78); al-Ghāshiya (88); al-Balad (90); al-Insān (76)

Ẓuhr and 'Ishā' Prayers: al-Shams (91); al-A'lā (87)

'Aṣr and Maghrib: al-Takāthur(102); al-Naṣr (110)

Ẓuhr, 'Aṣr and 'Ishā' on Fridays: first rak'at: al-Jumu'ah (62) and second rak'at: al-Munāfiqūn (63)

Fajr and Maghrib on Fridays: first rak'at: al-Jumu'ah (62) and second rak'at: al-'Ikhlāṣ (112)

All Prayers: first rak'at: al-Qadr (97) and second rak'at: al-'Ikhlāṣ (112)

Fajr Prayers on Mondays and Thursdays: first rak'at: al-Insān (76) and second rak'at: al-Ghāshiya (88)

46- Imagine you are writing what you recite

Some have suggested that imagining writing what they are reciting helps them concentrate in their recitation. With this technique, caution must be taken to concentrate on the meaning of the verses as well as the actual words. It is therefore essential to strike a balance between imagining writing what you are reciting and contemplating on what you are reciting, if one seeks to practise this suggestion.

47- Pause after reciting each verse

Pausing after recitation of each verse during the prayer helps to relax the mind and focus on the recitation. For instance, it is narrated from the sixth Imām, Imām al-Ṣādiq (as) that it is makrūh to read sūrah al-'Ikhlāṣ in a single breath:

يكره ان تقرأ قل هو الله احد في نفسٍ واحد

"It is not recommended (makrūh) to recite 'Say Allah is One' (sūrah al-'Ikhlāṣ) in one breath."[22]

Furthemore, it is recommended to pause after completing the recitation of sūrah al-Fātiḥah and before and after qunūt (invocation in the second rak'at).

48- Recite with a beautiful voice

Reciting the verses of the Holy Qur'ān in a beautiful voice gives the believer the ability to focus on the recitation and create a spiritual environment. It is narrated from the Prophet Muḥammad (saw) that he said:

إنّ من أجمل الجمال: الشعر الحسن، ونعم النعمة الصوت الحسن

"The most beautiful of all beautiful things are: the beautiful poem and the tone of a beautiful voice."[23]

Do not be discouraged if you feel that your voice is not beautiful. Attempt to make it beautiful by training your voice, especially when reading the Holy Qur'ān with the correct tajwīd[24] rules. Another narration from the Prophet (saw) says:

حسّنوا القرآن بأصواتكم، فإنّ الصوت الحسن يزيد القرآن حسناً

"Make the Qur'ān beautiful with your voices, as the beautiful voice increases the Qur'ān in beauty."[25]

49- Learn new invocations in qunut

In the second rak'ah of prayer, the believer who is aware of Allah, while recognising his own degradation and dependence, raises his hands to beseech the Lord, the Self-Sufficient, the Needless. While doing so, he should attempt to learn new invocations in his qunūt (invocation in prayer) that might help him connect to Allah (swt), while uttering the supplication and comprehending the meaning. For instance, the du'ā' might be personal, such as asking Allah to forgive his sins as he mentions them one by one (note that for the acceptance of the qunūt, the jurisprudential requirement is that the du'ā' should be recited in Arabic). Otherwise there are many short supplications that the believer can recite, including this recommended supplication:[26]

Du'ā' for Qunūt

لا إله إلا اللهُ الحَليمُ الكَريمُ، لا إله إلا اللهُ العَلِي العَظِيمُ سُبْحانَ الله رَبّ
السَموات السَبْعُ و رَبّ الارْضِينَ السَبْعُ ، وَما فِيهِنَّ وَما بَينَهُنَّ و رَبّ العَرْشِ
العَظِيم، والْحَمْدُ للهِ رَبِّ الْعَالَمِين

There is no God but Allah the Forbearing, the most Generous,
There is no God but Allah, the Exalted, the Mighty.
Glory be to Allah, the Lord of the seven heavens, and the Lord of the seven earths and what is inside and what is outside and Lord of the mighty Throne.
Praise be to Allah, the Lord of the worlds.

50- Understand the philosophy behind ruku'

In order to obtain spiritual fulfilment from al-rukūʿ, we must seek to understand the philosophy behind this position:

- The rukūʿ position is the preparation for complete and absolute surrender to the Omnipotent Lord. It is the stage when the believer extends out his neck and says in his heart uttering his pleas: *"Oh Allah, this is my neck, a core component of my body and is bowed before Your Glory and Majesty, and this is my head which is the essence of my existence, all at Your service. I provide these to Your Majesty with complete humbleness and submission to Your ever-lasting Power, begging You to accept me as a humble servant, and that Your Highness owns total and complete control over my life and affairs; I am under Your mercy. I seek to lose my life, my family, my wealth in Your way and for Your approval"*. This is the 'ādāb or the courtesy we must show when we are in that position.

- The rukūʿ is the glorification of Allah (swt). This is why we say when we are in the rukūʿ position: *"Glory be to my Lord, the Great, and praise belongs to Him"*. It is the position when the believer witnesses in his heart the veneration of the Lord, and the humbleness of the servant in the bowing position towards his Lord.

- The rukūʿ position is the preparation for the sujūd position. If you achieve the degree of submission of the rukūʿ, you would qualify for the sujūd as the rukūʿ is the sign of courtesy ('adab) and if performed in its proper manner, you will be ready to gain proximity to Allah in the sujūd.

- Hayder Jafari, an Islamic lecturer and researcher, wrote for this book:

> "Upon reflection, prayer can be viewed, symbolically, as a cycle of the whole life of an individual; wrapped up from

inception all the way to the return to Allah (swt) through death. Standing marks the start of life for the believer, and prostration in prayer marks the end. For the latter, the movement of prayer towards the sujūd portrays the return to earth at death in the same way as dying is the return to the Almighty Allah (swt). By taking this symbolic action of life in prayer, rukū' therefore acts as the bridge in the return to Allah (swt); marking the way towards the ultimate ending in sujūd."

51- Perform the recommended acts in ruku'

Some of the recommended acts to be performed in the rukū' position are: to raise your hand and recite *'Allāhu 'Akbar* (Allah is Greater) before and after rukū'; Put your knees all the way back, straighten your back and stretch your neck, recite the ṣalawāt before or after tasbīḥ and recite the following du'ā' before the tasbīḥ in rukū':[27]

Du'ā' for Rukū'

اللهم لك ركعت ولك أسلمت وعليك توكلت وأنت ربي، خشع لك قلبي

وسمعي وبصري وشعري وبشري ولحمي، ودمي ومخي وعصبي وعظامي وما

أقلته قدماي، غير مستنكف ولا مستكبر ولا مستحسر

O Allah, unto You I have bowed, and in You I have believed, and to You I have submitted My heart, hearing, sight, hair, skin, flesh, blood, mind, nerves, bones, tendons and what my feet carry are humbled before You, with no objection, arrogance and weariness.

In the bowing position, we supplicate to the Almighty by thanking Him for all the countless bounties He has bestowed on us, and acknowledging that all our body parts and organs are working in continuous gratitude towards Allah (swt). This feeling of incapability to completely thank the Almighty causes us to then offer sujūd before Him.

52-Alternate the tasbih in ruku' and sujud

It is common practice to recite *"Sūbḥāna rabbī al-aẓīmi wa bi-hamdih"* which means *"Glory be to my Lord, the Great, and praise belongs to Him"* when performing the rukū' and *"Subḥāna rabbī al-'alā wa bi-hamdih"* which means *"Glory be to my Lord, The Exalted, and praise belongs to Him"* when performing the sujūd. In order to prevent the brain becoming accustomed to repeating these tasbīḥ, it is recommended to alternatively recite one of the following tasbīḥ three times during rukū' *subḥān 'Allāh* or *'Allāhu 'Akbar* or *Al-ḥamdu li 'Allāh.*[28]

53- Praise Allah in qiyam for hearing your glorification

When in a state of rukū', we recite tasbīḥ and glorify the Almighty Allah (swt). When we stand upright after rukū' (qīyām), we recite "*Sami' Allāhu liman ḥamidah*" which means "*Allah (swt) hears those who glorify Him.*" Feel that Allah (swt) has indeed listened to your glorification, and recite this du'ā':[29]

Du'ā' for Qīyām

الحمد لله رب العالمين أهل الجبروت والكبرياء، والعظمة لله رب العالمين

Praise be to Allah, Lord of the worlds, worthy of Majesty and Magnificence, and All Power belongs to Allah, The Lord of the worlds.

54- Understand the philosophy of sujud

Comprehending the philosophy behind the act of prostrating to Allah no doubt provides the spiritual backbone needed to focus during prayers. Sujūd is the most rewarding position the believer can be in. It drives us closer to Allah (swt) as He states in chapter 96 verse 19.[30]

When prostrate, the believer is in a state of humbleness and humility in the presence of the Omnipotent Authority. The wider message is clear: attaining nearness to Allah in life can only occur while the believer expresses piety and humility towards his Creator. This can be achieved with sincere and submissive prostration to Allah, as arrogance and egoistic tendencies are suppressed and anxiety and stress are relieved during this unique Islamic act.

Furthermore, it is narrated that Imām 'Alī (as) was asked about the meaning of prostration, or sujūd and he described it beautifully:

معنى السجدة الأولى "تأويلها : اللهم إنك منها خلقتنا ": يعني من الأرض، وتأويل رفع رأسك: ومنها أخرجتنا " والسجدة الثانية: " واليها تعيدنا "، ورفع رأسك: " ومنها تخرجنا تارة اخرى

"The first sujūd means 'O Allah you have created us from it', meaning dust (we were dust in the beginning), and as I raise my head from sujūd, it means 'You took us out from it' (we came to the world from the dust). The second sujūd means 'From inside it You will take us back' (that we will again return to the earth), and as I raise my head from the second sujūd, it means 'From it You will raise us a second time' (i.e. on the Day of Resurrection I will rise up from the grave and be summoned)."[31]

This explanation refers to this verse in the Holy Qur'ān when it refers to dust:

مِنْهَا خَلَقْنَاكُمْ وَفِيهَا نُعِيدُكُمْ وَمِنْهَا نُخْرِجُكُمْ تَارَةً أُخْرَىٰ

From it did We create you, into it shall We return you, and from it shall We bring you forth another time. (20:55)

As you raise your head for the first time from the state of prostration, and as you have come to the world from dust, remember your sins and ask Allah (swt) for forgiveness before you do the second sujūd which is when you return to dust for the final time.

In addition to spiritual benefits, sujūd also has medical benefits according to Dr. Mohammed Karim Beebani:

> "Sajdah is a unique position as this is the only position in which the brain (or head) becomes lower than the heart and hence for the first time the blood gushes towards the brain with full force whereas in all other positions (even when lying down) the brain is above the heart when it has to work against gravity to send blood to the brain.
>
> In the position of sajdah due to the increased blood supply the brain receives more nourishment and it has good effect upon memory, vision, hearing, concentration, psyche and all other cognitive abilities. People who offer their prayers regularly have more will power and can cope with the difficulties of life in a much better manner. They have fewer incidences of headaches, psychological problems and other defects of cognitive functions."[32]

55- Prolong your sujud as much as you can

It is narrated from Imām ʿAlī (as):

لو يعلم المصلي ما يغشاه من جلال الله، مـا سره ان يرفـع رأسـه مـن السجود

"If the worshipper knew to what extent His (Allah's) magnificence surrounds him during prayer, he would never raise his head from the state of prostration."[33]

The Commander of the Faithful (as) here signifies the importance of prolonging our prostration to Allah (swt), by revealing to the believers the opportunity they are missing when they take prostration lightly and without sincerity. The state of prostration to Allah (swt) teaches us humility, obedience, piety and humbleness. Most importantly, it takes us nearer to Allah (swt) than in any other possible state.

It is also narrated from Imām al-Ṣādiq (as) that he heard his father, Imām al-Bāqir (as), in the mosque one night alone in prostration, reciting the following:[34]

Duʿā' for Sujūd

سبحانك اللهم أنت ربي حقا حقا سجدت لك يا رب تعبدا ورقا، اللهم إن عملي ضعيف فضاعفه لي، اللهم قني عذابك يوم تبعث عبادك وتب علي إنك أنت التواب الرحيم

Glorified be You, O Allah. You are my Lord most definitely.
There is no God but Allah, I prostrate to You, O Lord, and worship You and serve You.
O Allah, my actions are weak so strengthen it for me,
O Allah protect me from Your punishment on the day You raise up Your servants, and forgive me,
as you are Relenting and Merciful.

56- Recite du'a between the two sujud and during and after sujud

It is recommended to recite salwāt tasbīḥ during sujūd, du'ā' before the tasbīḥ, and during the last sujūd of the prayer.[35]

Du'ā' before tasbīḥ while in sujūd

اللهم لك سجدت وبك آمنت ولك أسلمت وعليك توكلت وأنت ربي سجد وجهي

للذي خلقه وشق سمعه وبصره والحمد لله رب العالمين

تبارك الله أحسن الخالقين

Oh Allah, To you I have prostrated and in You I have believed and to You I have submitted and in You I put my trust and You are my Lord, my face prostrates to Him who created it and brought forth its hearing and seeing. Praise be to Allah the Lord of the worlds, blessed be Allah the best of Creators.

Du'ā' after the last sujūd

يا خير المسؤولين ويا خير المعطين ارزقني وارزق عيالي من فضلك

فإنك ذوالفضل العظيم

O You Who are the best from whom people seek their needs, and O You Who are the best bestower of gifts! Give me and the members of my family sustenance with Your grace. Undoubtedly You possess the greatest grace.

Du'ā' in between the two sujūd

اللهم اغفر لي وارحمني وأجرني وادفع عني ، فإني لما أنزلت إلي من خير فقير ،

تبارك الله رب العالمين

Oh Allah, forgive me and have mercy on me, compensate me and defend me, I stand in need of whatever good You may send down to me. Blessed be Allah, the Lord of the worlds.

57- Contemplate on the meaning of the tasbih in the third and/or fourth rak'at

As we move to the third and/or forth rak'ah, we recite this tasbīḥ three times:[36]

سبحان اللهِ والحمدُ للهِ ولا إله إلاّ اللهُ واللهُ أكبر

"Glory be to Allah, all praise is for Allah, there is no God but Allah and Allah is thee Greatest"

To attain the maximum benefit of this recitation, it is important to contemplate on the meaning of the tasbīḥ. The word subḥān is defined by Arabic litterateurs as 'al-tanzīh' which is translated to mean 'transcendence'. When we say *"subḥān 'Allāh"* we are saying *"O Allah, You are transcendent above all creators and creations and You are transcendent above all time and space and You are transcendent above all imperfection and deficiency as all Your actions are holy and free from evil and injustice"*. This meaning is referred to briefly in the Holy Qur'ān when Allah (swt) refutes the claims of the ignorant and the disbelievers:

قُلْ لَوْ كَانَ مَعَهُ آلِهَةٌ كَمَا يَقُولُونَ إِذًا لَابْتَغَوْا إِلَىٰ ذِي الْعَرْشِ سَبِيلًا

سُبْحَانَهُ وَتَعَالَىٰ عَمَّا يَقُولُونَ عُلُوًّا كَبِيرًا

Say: If there were with Him gods as they say, then certainly they would have been able to seek a way to the Lord of power. Transcendent is He and exalted be He in high exaltation above what they say. (17:42-43)

As we continue and say *"wa al-ḥamdu li 'Allāh"* we should differentiate between the words 'al-ḥamd' and 'al-shukr' as they are both often translated as 'praise'. 'al-shukr' is used to thank Allah (swt) for a specific grace or bounty that Allah has bestowed, whereas 'al-ḥamd' is a more general form of thankfulness where you send your gratitude to Him for all the gifts and graces He has bestowed on you. For example, you may want to thank Allah (swt) for the birth of your child, and by saying *"shukran li-Allāh"* you have praised Allah for the safe delivery of your child but if you say *"al-ḥamdu li 'Allāh"* you go beyond that and praise Allah for all His bounties and blessings He has provided.

Finally as you utter "*Wa lā 'ilaha 'illā Allāh wa Allāhu 'akbar*" you are clearly and firmly stating your monotheistic belief by sincerely believing He is the only one and no one is greater than Him as well as affirming that He is the Omnipotent and the Omniscient Lord of the worlds and the universe.[37]

58- Focus on the true meanings of the taslim

When you recite the taslīm (at the sitting position after prostration), send salām (greetings of peace) and bid farewell to the prayer the way a mother bids farewell to a beloved. Take your time and feel the benefits of this spiritual journey that you have just undertaken and the disappointment that is coming to an end. As you bid farewell with the taslīm, you are attaining security from the trials of this world and exemption from the tortures of the Hereafter.

As you recite the last obligatory salām: *"Asalāmu 'alykum wa raḥmatullāh"* which means *"Allah's peace, blessings and mercy be upon you"*; know that you are sending your salām to the prophets, the Ahl al-Bayt (as), the true believers - deceased or alive - the angels and the jinn, and feel the warmth and blessings of their reply to you as you end this spiritual journey of prayer.

59- Imagine every part of your body will bear witness to the oneness of Allah (swt)

As you praise Allah (swt) in the tashahhud, have no doubt in your heart that you bear witness that there is no god but Allah and imagine every part of your body to bear witness to His Oneness. Feel the reality of tawḥīd spread through your organs, as each organ has a share of the tawḥīd.

Regarding tashahhud, it is narrated in *Miṣbāḥ al-Sharīʿah*:

> "The tashahhud is praise of Allah. Be a slave to Him in your innermost being, fearful and humble to Him in action as you are His bondsman by word and claim. Join the truthfulness of your tongue to the pure truthfulness of your innermost being. He created you a slave and commanded you to worship Him with your heart, your tongue and your limbs. Realise your enslavement to Him by His lordship over you. Know that the forelocks of creation are all in His hand. Creatures possess neither breath nor sight except by His power and will: they are incapable of bringing forth the least thing in His kingdom, unless it is by His permission and will."[38]

60- Remember the greatness of the Prophet (saw) and his progeny during taslim

As you send your salutations upon the Holy Prophet (saw) and his family during taslīm, remember that they are the people of the Right Path and you aspire to follow that righteous path as long as you are alive. In addition, if the ṣalawāt is recited sincerely, then the believer should expect ten salutations sent to them from Allah (swt) as narrated by this ḥādīth from the Holy Prophet (saw):

من صلى علي مرة صلى الله عليه عشرا و من صلى علي عشرا صلى الله

عليه مائة مرة

"Whoever recites one salutation upon me, Allah will reciprocate ten salutations upon the reciter and whoever recites ten salutations upon me, Allah will reciprocate this with one hundred salutations"[39]

Moreover, the importance of the ṣalawāt is emphasised further to the extent that if you hear the name of the Holy Prophet (saw) while reciting the verses during prayer, it is recommended to send your salutations to him and his family at that stage of the prayer.

The following is a narration from Imām al-Ṣādiq (as) that supports this:

عن عبد الله بن سنان قال: سألت أبا عبد الله عليه السلام عن الرجل يذكر النبي صلى الله عليه وآله وهو في الصلاة المكتوبة إما راكعا وإما ساجدا فيصلي عليه وهو على تلك الحال؟ فقال: " نعم إن الصلاة على نبي الله صلى الله عليه وآله كهيئة التكبير والتسبيح، وهي عشر حسنات يبتدرها ثمانية عشر ملكا أيهم يبلغها إياه

"'Abd Allāh ibn Sinān said: 'I asked 'Abū 'Abdallāh (Imām al-Ṣādiq) about a man who mentions the Prophet during prayer in rukū' or in sujūd [positions] and sends his salutations upon the Prophet and his family.' He said: 'Yes, the salutations upon the Prophet and his family are like the takbīr and the tasbīḥ, and it holds ten rewards [ḥasanāt] which is accelerated by eighteen angels who will deliver it (the ṣalawāt) to the Prophet."[40]

61- Recite the recommended du'a during the tashahhud and taslim

It is recommended to prolong your tashahhud and taslīm in glorification of Allah (swt) and His Prophet (saw) and his family, and to increase your attention with new invocations. The following du'ā' is suggested during tashahhud and taslīm:

If you are praying three or more rak'ah, recite the following (in Arabic) after the second rak'ah:[41]

Recitation After Second Rak'at

بسم الله وبالله والحمد لله وخير الاسماء لله ، أشهد أن لا إله إلا الله وحده

لا شريك له ، وأشهد أن محمدا عبده ورسوله أرسله بالحق بشيرا ونذيرا بين

يدي الساعة ، أشهد أنك نعم الرب ، وأن محمدا نعم الرسول ،

اللهم صل على محمد وآل محمد ، وتقبل شفاعته في امته وارفع درجته

In the name of Allah and by Allah, and praise be to Allah, and the best names are for Allah. I bear witness that there is no god but Allah, He alone, there is no partner to Him, and that Muḥammad is His servant and His messenger, He sent him with the truth giving tidings and portents ahead of the Hour,
I testify that You are truly an excellent Lord and that Muḥammad is truly an excellent messenger,
O Allah bless Muḥammad and the family of Muḥammad and accept his intercession for his 'ummah and raise his degree.

Then praise Allah twice or three times (for example, by saying, *"Al-ḥamdu li 'Allāh"* meaning *"Praise be to Allah"*) and get up for the third rak'at. If you are finishing off the prayer, then recite the following (in Arabic) from the start of your tashahhud:[42]

Recitation during Tashahhud

بسم الله وبالله والحمد لله وخير الاسماء لله ، أشهد أن لا إله إلا الله وحده لا شريك له ، وأشهد أن محمدا عبده ورسوله ، أرسله بالحق بشيرا ونذيرا بين يدي الساعة ، أشهد أنك نعم الرب وأن محمدا نعم الرسول ، التحيات لله والصلوات الطاهرات الطيبات الزاكيات الغاديات الرائحات السابغات الناعمات ماطاب وزكى وطهر وخلص وصفا فللّه ، أشهد أن لا إله إلا الله وحده لا شريك له ، وأشهد أن محمدا عبده ورسوله ، أرسله بالحق بشيرا ونذيرا بين يدى الساعة ، أشهد أن ربي نعم الرب وأن محمدا نعم الرسول ، وأشهد أن الساعة آتية لا ريب فيها وأن الله يبعث من في القبور ، الحمد لله الذي هدانا لهذا وما كنا لنهتدي لو لا أن هدانا الله ، الحمد لله رب العالمين ، اللهم صل على محمد وآل محمد ، وبارك على محمد وآل محمد ، وسلم على محمد وآل محمد ، وترحم على محمد وآل محمد ، كما صليت وباركت وترحمت على إبراهيم وآل إبراهيم إنك حميد مجيد ، اللهم صل على محمد وآل محمد ، واغفر لنا ولاخواننا الذين سبقونا بالايمان ، ولا تجعل في قلوبنا غلا للذين آمنوا ربنا إنك رؤوف رحيم ، اللهم صل على محمد وآل محمد وامنن علي بالجنة وعافني من النار ، اللهم صل على محمد وآل محمد ، واغفر للمؤمنين والمؤمنات ولا تزد الظالمين إلا تبارا السلام عليك أيها النبي ورحمة الله وبركاته ، السلام على أنبياء الله ورسله ، السلام على جبرئيل وميكائيل والملائكة المقربين ، السلام على محمد بن عبدالله خاتم النبيين لا نبي بعده ، والسلام علينا وعلى عباد الله الصالحين

السلام عليكم ورحمة الله وبركاته

In the name of Allah and by Allah, and praise be to Allah, and the best names are for Allah, I testify that there is no god but Allah, He alone, there is no partner for Him, and I testify that Muḥammad is His messenger and His servant, He sent him by the truth, giving tidings and portents before the Hour, I testify that You truly are an excellent Lord and that Muḥammad truly is an excellent messenger, Salutations are for Allah and the Pure, Good, Righteous, morning, afternoon, abundant, delicate prayers are for Allah. What is good and pure and unalloyed and clear is for Allah, and I testify that my Lord is truly an excellent Lord and that Muḥammad is truly an excellent messenger, I testify that the Hour is coming, there is no doubt in it, and that Allah will resurrect whoever is in the graves Praise be to Allah who guided us to this, and we would not be guided had Allah not guided us; praise be to Allah Lord of the worlds. O Allah bless Muḥammad and the family of Muḥammad, and send benediction upon Muḥammad and the family of Muḥammad, and send peace upon Muḥammad and the family of Muḥammad, and have mercy upon Muḥammad and the family of Muḥammad, as you have blessed and sent benediction and had mercy upon Ibrāhīm and the family of Ibrāhīm, verily You are Praiseworthy, Glorious. O Allah bless Muḥammad and the family of Muḥammad, and forgive us and our brethren who preceded us in the faith, and do not place in our hearts malice to those who have believed in our Lord, verily You are compassionate, Merciful. O Allah bless Muḥammad and the family of Muḥammad, and grant me the Garden and save me from the Fire. O Allah bless Muḥammad and the family of Muḥammad and forgive the believing men and women and whoso entered my house believing and the believing men and women, and do not increase the wrongdoers [or oppressors] but in perdition. Peace be upon you O Prophet and the mercy of Allah and his blessings. Peace be upon the prophets of Allah and His messengers. Peace be upon Jibrā'īl and Mīkā'īl and the angels brought near. Peace be upon Muḥammad bin `Abdullah, the Seal of the Prophets, there is no prophet after him, and peace be upon us and upon the servants of Allah, the righteous ones. Allah's peace, mercy and blessings be upon you.

62- If you lose concentration, bounce back fast

If your focus during the prayer slips away, but you know which ra'ka you are in,[43] attempt to bounce back and use this as a warning and attention alarm to concentrate on the remainder of your prayer. If you are reciting from the Holy Qur'ān and realise that you have lost concentration for the last few seconds, pause, take a deep breath and then continue with your recitation with contemplation on the meanings of the remainder of the sūrah. Do not allow one or two slips in concentration to ruin this spiritual journey as you might otherwise begin to get frustrated and lose hope.

63- Pray at a measured pace

It is often the case that we are in a hurry and need to complete our prayer quickly. However, it is unlikely that we will be able to concentrate during that prayer. Generally, if we perform tasks slowly, we tend to gain a deeper focus, appreciation, enjoyment and make fewer mistakes. One who has a true appreciation of whom he is facing in his prayer will be prevented from rushing and will seek to attain spirituality from his Lord by continuing at a measured pace.

64- Fix your gaze during prayer

When the believer stands in front of his Lord, he should stand upright in stillness and modesty, not raising his head as if he is standing in front of his enemy and competitor, and not exaggerate in lowering his head as if he is upset or sad. He should fix his gaze towards the point where he places his forehead while in prostration and places his hands beside his hips in complete respect and submission. His gaze should be fixed during the rukūʿ position and also as he ascends towards the sujūd:

الَّذِي يَرَاكَ حِينَ تَقُومُ وَتَقَلُّبَكَ فِي السَّاجِدِينَ

Who sees you when you stand up. And thy movements among those who prostrate themselves. (26:218-219)

Researchers confirm that fixing the gaze on a small object aids concentration. See point 98 for further details.

65- Shed some tears during prayer while contemplating non-wordly affairs

Some 'aḥādīth report that it is recommended to shed tears in prayer while contemplating non-worldly affairs (deliberate crying due to worldly matters invalidates prayers accroding to Sayid Yazid, and as commented by Ayatollah Sistani). For instance, one may shed tears when contemplating Allah's existence, the verses of the Qurʿān, or Paradise and Hellfire.

It is narrated that Imām al-Ṣādiq (as) was asked about whether shedding tears during prayer voids the prayer.

و عن أَبي حنيفةَ قال: سألتُ أَبا عبد الله (ع) عن البكاء في الصَّلاةِ أ يقطعُ

الصَّلاةَ؟ فقال: إن بكى لذكرِ جنَّةٍ أو نارٍ فذلكَ هـو أفضـلُ الأعـمال في الصَّـلاة

وإن كان ذكر ميتاً له فصلاته فاسدة

"From 'Abū Ḥanīfah, he said: I asked 'Abū Abdallāh (as) whether shedding tears during prayer will make the prayer void? He said: If he sheds tears when mentioning Paradise or Hellfire, then this is the best acts of prayer but if he mentions a dead person known to him and sheds tears (on the demise of the dead person) then his prayer will become void."[44]

The Ahl al-Bayt (as) were known to shed tears in their prayers, as a means of getting closer to Allah (swt), to ask Allah (swt) to grant mercy to a community and to enlighten their heart with complete submission to Him. It is narrated from Imām 'Alī (as):

البكاء من خشية الله ينير القلب

"Shedding tears when submitting to Allah lightens the heart."[45]

It is reported that Imām al-Sajjād (as) used to repeat the verse (1:4): "*mālik yawm al-dīn*" which means, *"Master of the Day of Judgment"* during his prayer. While reciting, he would collapse and when he lifted his head from prostration it was as if he had inserted his head into a bucket of water due to the flood of tears he would shed during the prayer.[46]

However, it is important that one should not merely cry for the sake of it. The tears should flow automatically as a result of fear of Allah (swt)'s Justice, and as a consequence of our desperation for His Mercy and Forgiveness.

66- Avoid continuous doubting and obsessive repetition of verses

Continuous doubting and obsessive repetition of verses can have a disruptive effect on the prayer. It focuses the believer's attention disproportionately on the literal words recited and less on the meaning or spiritual essence. The scholars say that if you continuously have doubts in your prayer, you should ignore such doubts and continue your prayer as normal. It is narrated from Imām al-Bāqir (as):

إذا كثر عليك السهو فامض في صلاتك فإنه يوشك أن يدعك إنما هو من الشيطان

"When doubts in the prayer become too frequent, do not give heed to them, and regard the prayer to be correct. It is hoped that this state will leave you, as Shayṭān causes it."[47]

67- Face the ground in humility

As you face Allah (swt), face Him as a submissive servant. Bow your head whilst standing and sitting and release any arrogance and pride from within you. Understand your worthlessness in front of Him by lowering your head like any creature would in front of its master.

To sit in a humble way, the following are some recommended acts to perform while you are in the sitting position during tashahhud and taslīm:

- Sit in a ṭuruq way; this is when you sit on your left thigh, resting the back of your left foot on top of the right foot.[48]

-Keep your hands on your lap, with fingers close to each other.[49]

-Practise deep breathing techniques; see point 94.

Conclusion

The objective of this chapter is to take the reader through various methods that may help in connecting the heart and mind to Allah (swt) during prayer. Remembering these points and practising them may transform our prayer into a conversation with the Lord and an overflowing river in which we can purify our own souls. It is narrated from the Prophet Muḥammad (saw) that he said:

إنما مثل الصلاة فيكم كمثل السري وهو النهر على باب أحدكم يخرج
إليه في اليوم والليلة يغتسل منه خمس مرات، فلم يبق الدرن مع
الغسل خمس مرات، ولم تبق الذنوب مع الصلاة خمس مرات

"The example of prayers is like that of a river outside one's house, into which a believer immerses themselves five times a day. Upon this, no impurities remain on their bodies. Likewise, prayers clean your soul of sins five times a day"[50]

Endnotes

1. Kashani, *al-Mahajjah al-Bayḍā'*, vol. 1, p.385.
2. Isfahani, *Ṣalāh (Prayer): The Mode of Divine Proximity and Recognition*, Section on 'Adhān and 'Iqāmah. See [http://www.al-islam.org/salat-prayer-mode-divine-proximity-and-recognition-ayatullah-mirza-mahdi-isfahani] 16/03/2014.
3. Yazdi, M. Comments by al-Sistānī. A. *al-Urwatul Withqa*. Part Two, p. 145.
4. Khomeini, *'Ādāb al-Ṣalāt: The Disciplines of the Prayer,* Discourse Four, Chapter 5, p. 443.
5. al-Shirazi. *Al-'Amthāl fī Tafsīr al-Qur'ān,* vol. 1, p. 29.
6. al-Ṭabrasī, *Majma' al-Bayān.* vol. 1, p. 54.
7. al-Ṣadūq, *Man Lā Yaḥḍuruh al-Faqīh*, vol. 1, p. 310.
8. al-Ṭabrasī, *Majma' al-Bayān.* vol. 1, p. 48.
9. The exegesis of sūrah al-Fātiḥah was inspired by: al-Shirazi. *Al-'Amthāl fī Tafsīr al-Qur'ān,* vol. 1, p. 17-49, Exegesis of sūrah al-Fātiḥah; Qarā'atī, M. *A Commentary on Prayer*, p. 135; and Imanī, K.F. *An Enlightening Commentary into the Light of the Holy Qur'ān*, vol. 1, p. 33.
10. Note that martyrs is one of a few other interpretations of the word 'shuhadā', One other meaning is 'witnesses'.
11. al-Shirazi. *Al-'Amthāl fī Tafsīr al-Qur'ān,* vol. 1, p. 47.
12. The exegesis of sūrah al-'Ikhlāṣ was inspired by: al-Shirazi. *Al-'Amthāl fī Tafsīr al-Qur'ān,* vol. 20. p. 425-436, Exegesis of sūrah al-'Ikhlāṣ; and Qarā'atī, M. *A Commentary on Prayer*, p. 173
13. al-Ṭayālisī, *Musnad Ibn Dawūd al-Ṭayālisī*, p. 131.
14. al-Kulaynī, *Al-Kāfī*, vol. 2, p. 455.
15. Imanī, K.F. *An Enlightening Commentary into the Light of the Holy Qur'ān,* vol. 20, p. 298-299.
16. al-Sharīf al-Raḍī, *Nahj al-Balāghah*, Sermon 186.
17. Yazdi, M. Comments by al-Sistānī. A. *al-Urwatul Withqa*. Part Two. p. 146.

18. Ibid.
19. al-Kulaynī, *al-Kāfī*, vol. 1, p. 91.
20. It is best to avoid sūrah al-'Alaq (96) as it has a compulsory sajdah. Also see jurisprudential rulings regarding combining sūrah 93 and 94 and combining sūrah 105 and 106.
21. Yazdi, M. Comments by al-Sistānī. A. *al-Urwatul Withqa*. Part Two. p. 146.
22. al-Kulaynī, *al-Kāfī*, vol. 2, p. 451.
23. al-Kulaynī, *al-Kāfī*, vol. 2, p. 615.
24. Women can only recite the verses loud during prayer in front of a mahram.
25. al-Ṣadūq, *'Uyūn Akhbār al-Riḍā*, vol. 1, p. 75.
26. Yazdi, M. Comments by al-Sistānī. A. *al-Urwatul Withqa*. Part Two. p. 186.
27. Yazdi, M. Comments by al-Sistānī. A. *al-Urwatul Withqa*. Part Two. p. 157.
28. Ibid, p. 150.
29. Yazdi, M. Comments by al-Sistānī. A. *al-Urwatul Withqa*. Part Two. p. 157.
30. This is a verse of obligatory sajdah, thus not mentioned here.
31. al-Ṣadūq, *'Ilāl al-Sharāyi'*, vol. 4, p. 336.
32. Saudi Gazette, July 7, 2000.
33. al-Ṣadūq, *al-Khiṣāl*, p. 632.
34. al-Kulaynī, *al-Kāfī*, vol. 3, p. 323.
35. Yazdi, M. Comments by al-Sistānī. A. *al-Urwatul Withqa*. Part Two. p. 167-169.
36. It is wajib to recite this only once; three times is mustaḥab.
37. Refer to exegesis of sūrah al-'Ikhlāṣ in this chapter for a more comprehensive meaning of The Oneness of Allah (swt).
38. Hā'irī, *Miṣbāḥ al-Sharī'ah*: (The Lantern of the Path), p. 53.
39. al-Sabzawari, Ja'ami Al-Akhbaar, Section 28, p. 153.
40. al-Kulaynī, *al-Kāfī*, vol. 3, p. 322.

41. Yazdi, M. Comments by al-Sistānī. A. *al-Urwatul Withqa*. Part Two. p. 179.
42. Ibid, p. 179-180. Translation from: [http://www.tashayyu.org/hadiths/minhaj-waqifa/salat/tashahhud/chapter-3] 18/03/2014.
43. If you do not know which ra'ka you are in, you must apply the appropriate rulings of al-shakk fi al-ṣalāh (doubt in prayer). Refer to the jurisprudential books for more information.
44. al-Tūsī, *Tahdhīb al-'Aḥkām*, vol. 2, p. 317.
45. Mirzā al-Nūrī, *Mustadrak al-Wasā'il*, vol. 11, p. 245.
46. al-Kulaynī, *al-Kāfī*, vol. 2, p. 440.
47. al-Kulaynī, *al-Kāfī*, vol. 3, p. 359.
48. Yazdi, M. Comments by al-Sistānī. A. *al-Urwatul Withqa*. Part Two. p. 182.
49. Ibid.
50. al-Ṣadūq, *Man Lā Yaḥḍuruh al-Faqīh*, vol. 1, p. 211.

Chapter 5: The Consequence

The prayer is an *experience* – and the journey back from meeting the Lord is as crucial as the journey towards Him. Therefore, there are many steps a believer can take immediately after the prayer to maximise the spiritual benefits of the prayer. These include pre-occupying oneself following the ritual prayer with supplications, remembrance of Allah (swt), recitation of the Qur'ān and other recommended rituals such as reflection, contemplation and asking for forgiveness.

In this chapter:

68. Continue to remember Allah after prayer
69. Ask Allah for forgiveness
70. Perform two sajdāt of gratitude
71. Assess how well you concentrated after each prayer
72. Contemplate in between combined prayers

68- Continue to remember Allah after prayer

Prayer can be described as an act of remembering Allah (swt) as Allah (swt) informs Prophet Mūsa (as):

وَأَقِمِ الصَّلَاةَ لِذِكْرِي

And keep up prayer for My remembrance. (20:14)

In fact, remembering Allah (swt) does not merely mean uttering His name by tongue, but 'remembering' Him and His glory in our heart. The reward is that the heart will be assured and tranquil:

الَّذِينَ آمَنُوا وَتَطْمَئِنُّ قُلُوبُهُمْ بِذِكْرِ اللَّهِ أَلَا بِذِكْرِ اللَّهِ تَطْمَئِنُّ الْقُلُوبُ

"Those who have faith, and whose hearts find rest in the remembrance of Allah.' Look! The hearts find rest in Allah's remembrance! (13:28)

In another verse, Allah (swt) describes those believers who remember Him as having fearful hearts:

إِنَّمَا الْمُؤْمِنُونَ الَّذِينَ إِذَا ذُكِرَ اللَّهُ وَجِلَتْ قُلُوبُهُمْ وَإِذَا تُلِيَتْ عَلَيْهِمْ آيَاتُهُ
زَادَتْهُمْ إِيمَانًا وَعَلَىٰ رَبِّهِمْ يَتَوَكَّلُونَ

The faithful are only those whose hearts tremble [with awe] when Allah is mentioned, and when His signs are recited to them, they increase their faith, and who put their trust in their Lord. (8:2)

According to the above two verses, the significance of the remembrance of Allah (swt) entails that He instils two seemingly opposing feelings in the believer's heart: fear and tranquillity. A true and humble believer's heart will tremble with fear due to his sins and shortcomings while simultaneously being tranquil in the face of conflicting desires and worldly pleasures.

One other benefit of remembering Allah is the joy and happiness that it brings to the heart, as Allah (swt) says in sūrah al-Jumu'ah:

فَإِذَا قُضِيَتِ الصَّلَاةُ فَانْتَشِرُوا فِي الْأَرْضِ وَابْتَغُوا مِنْ فَضْلِ اللَّهِ وَاذْكُرُوا اللَّهَ كَثِيرًا لَعَلَّكُمْ تُفْلِحُونَ

And when the prayer is finished disperse through the land and seek Allah's grace, and remember Allah greatly so that you may be felicitous. (62:10)

To be contextual to the verse cited, where 'disperse' and 'seek grace' and 'remember Allah' are linked, one must return to their normal affairs with a heightened sense of perception of the remembrance of Allah, which will also help to perpetuate the 'spiritual high' gained from the prayer.

To achieve this further, it is advisable to spend time after prayer reading the Qur'ān, reciting the recommended du'ā' after prayers (ta'qībāt), reciting ṣalawāt on the Prophet (saw) and his family, performing tasbīḥ (such as tasbīḥāt al-Zahrā (as)) or contemplating the creation of Allah (swt). This will certainly help maintain the spiritual high gained from the prayers for a longer period, and makes it easier to continue that state into the next prayer.

69- Ask Allah for forgiveness

After completing your prayer, take a few minutes to talk to Allah (swt) in your own language. Mention your sins, acknowledge your faults and ask Allah (swt) for forgiveness. Know that Allah (swt) knows your problems and calamities, He wants you to mention them to Him and ask Him sincerely to help you and He will answer. If you feel your prayer lacked concentration, ask Him to help you improve your concentration in the next prayer. You may like to recite the following du'ā' after completing your prayer:[1,2]

Du'ā' after Completing the Prayer

الهي هذه صلاتي صليتها لالحاجة منك إليها, ولا رغبة منك فيها,إلا تعظيما
وطاعة وإجابة لك إلى مأمرتني به,الهي إن كان فيها خلل أو نقص من ركوعها
أو سجودها فلا تؤاخذني وتفضل على بالقبول والغفران برحمتك ياارحم
الراحمين وياخير الغافرين وصلى على محمدا وآله الطاهرين.

My Allah, the prayer I have just prayed, was not to put forth any demand before You,
nor was there any self-seeking desire to reach You through it.
It was nothing but praise, obedience and surrender unto You, in order to carry out that which You have commanded.
My Allah, If there was a break in continuity (disturbance of mind) or a shortcoming, while making the intention, or while standing, bowing down, or prostrating in adoration, do not catch hold of me, (but) be so kind as to bestow a favour on me - by affording me through Your mercy absolution and acceptance, O the Most Merciful. With your mercy, O Most Merciful of those who have mercy. O the Best of Forgivers.
Greetings and salutations on the Prophet (saw)
and his pure progeny.

Duʿā' for Forgiveness

اَللّـهُمَّ إنَّ مَغْفِرَتَكَ اَرْجى مِنْ عَمَلى وَاِنَّ رَحْمَتِكَ أوْسَعُ مِنْ ذَنْبي اَللّـهُمَّ إن كانَ
ذَنبي عِنْدَكَ عَظيماً فَعَفْوُكَ اَعْظَمُ مِنْ ذَنْبي اَللّـهُمَّ إنْ لَمْ اَكُنْ أهْلاً أنْ اَبْلُغَ
رَحْمَتُكَ فرحمتك اَهْلٌ اَنْ تَبْلُغَني وَتَسَعَني لاِنَّها وَسِعَتْ كُلَّ شَيْء بِرَحْمَتِكَ
يا اَرْحَمَ الرّاحِمينَ

O Allah, indeed, Your forgiveness is more to be hoped for than my deeds; certainly Your mercy is more deep and far-reaching compared to my faults and mistakes.
O Allah if my errors, in the matter of Your laws, are grave in nature, Your pardon is more substantial and well-known than my transgressions.
O Allah, if I'm not worthy of receiving Your Mercy; Your Mercy is large enough to receive me, as it encompasses everything, through Your kindness.
With Your Mercy O Most Merciful of those who have mercy.

70- Perform two sajdat of gratitude

It is recommended to prostrate to Allah (swt) in gratitude twice (sajdāt al-shukr) after every prayer. This is the closest position a believer can get to Allah (swt) so if time permits, say *"Al-ḥamdu li 'Allāh"*; *"Praise be to Allah"* and thank Allah by saying, *"Shukran li-Allāh"* in every sajdah at least three times (increase if you have time). Between these two prostrations, it is recommended to rub your forehead and cheeks in the dust as narrated by Imām al-Ṣādiq (as):[3]

إذا ذكر أحدكم نعمة الله عزوجل فليضع خده على التراب شكرا لله

"If any of you remember the bounties of Allah (swt), he should place his cheeks on dust thanking Allah (swt)."[4]

Giving thanks to Allah (swt) has many rewards. Allah (swt) states in sūrah Luqmān that by thanking Him, one is in fact benefiting himself as Allah is All-Sufficient and not in need of the believer's gratitude:

وَلَقَدْ آتَيْنَا لُقْمَانَ الْحِكْمَةَ أَنِ اشْكُرْ لِلَّهِ ۚ وَمَنْ يَشْكُرْ فَإِنَّمَا يَشْكُرُ لِنَفْسِهِ

ۖ وَمَنْ كَفَرَ فَإِنَّ اللَّهَ غَنِيٌّ حَمِيدٌ

Certainly We gave Luqmān wisdom, saying, 'Give thanks to Allah; and whoever gives thanks, gives thanks only for his own sake. And whoever is ungrateful, [let him know that] Allah is indeed All-Sufficient, All-Laudable.' (31:12)

Moreover, Imām al-Riḍhā (as) narrates that if the prayer performed was devoid of concentration and submission then the prostration of thanksgiving will help perfect it:

السجدة بعد الفريضة شكرا لله تعالى ذكره على ما وفق العبد من أداء

فريضة، وأدنى ما يجزي فيها من القول أن يقال: "شكر لله شكرا لله" ثلاث

مرات، قلت: فما معنى شكرا لله؟ قال (ع): يقول هذه السجدة مني
شكرا لله على ما وفقني له من خدمته وأداء فرضه، والشكر موجب
للزيادة، فإن كان في الصلاة تقصير تم بهذه السجدة

"The prostration after an obligatory prayer is an expression of thanking Almighty Allah for granting His servant success to carry out his duty towards Him. The least of what can be said while prostrating is to repeat the following words three times: 'Thanks be to Allah.' 'What is the meaning of Thanks be to Allah?' the reporter asked, and the Imām (as) answered, 'It means that this prostration is a thanksgiving from me to Almighty Allah for the success that He has granted me to serve Him and carry out my duty towards Him. Verily, thanking Almighty Allah increases graces and grants more success to obey Him. If it happens that a prayer is still imperfect and the supererogatory prayer has not covered that imperfection, then this thanksgiving prostration will perfect it."[5]

There are three types of gratitude. The first is gratitude of the tongue that we use to praise Allah (swt) for His blessings and grace on us. The second is the gratitude of the heart, where the heart is thankful to Allah for witnessing the constant recognition of His blessings. The third is the gratitude of the limbs as they are enabled to always obey Allah and are kept away from transgressions. For example, being able to use the eyes to look at what is ḥalāl, and being able to divert the gaze away from the ḥarām, and for the tongue to be empowered to speak the truth, and refrain from lying and backbiting.

Luqmān (as) practised all these three types of gratitude as he possessed the 'ḥikmah' or wisdom, which constitutes the noble knowledge, correct understanding, pure morals, piety, fear of Allah and guidance. Through these attributes, one is able to be grateful to Allah (swt) in the three ways.

71- Assess how well you concentrated after each prayer

If you feel that you struggle with concentration, try to assess your level of concentration after each prayer. Assess sincerely and critically whether your concentration is improving or worsening. Try to make small improvements every week and do a final assessment of your concentration at the end of the week. Try to score yourself out of ten and be as critical of yourself as you can. Keep the scores in a secret place so that this remains a genuine critical assessment of your prayer. After a month, add up your scores and if your concentration is improving then whatever you are practising is working and you should continue with that method. If your score is relatively low, or is becoming worse or remains unchanged you should revise the methods used, if any, to focus in prayer and evaluate their efficacy.

However, remain optimistic and be patient until you start to improve. If your concentration in one of the five daily prayers is weak, then aim to strengthen it in the next. Never give up attempting to improve your concentration since, as with anything else, concentration is improved through practice and struggle. Once you are successful in getting closer to Him, He will come even closer to you as narrated in this ḥadīth al-qudsī:

من تقرب إلي شبراً تقربت إليه ذراعاً

"And whoever draws near to Me by a span's length, I will draw near him by an arm's length."[6]

72- Contemplate in between combined prayers

If you decide to combine the ẓuhr and ʿaṣr, or the maghrib and ʿishāʾ prayers, spend the time in between the prayers in contemplation, reading the Holy Qurʿān or duʿāʾ and do not distract yourself with other worldly issues. Without thinking, it is possible to may find youself chatting or using mobile phones in between the prayers.

If concentration in the ẓuhr prayer, for example, was not sufficient, then spend a few moments preparing for the ʿaṣr prayer in silent contemplation. Distractions will eventually create obstructive thoughts that will linger on into the prayer and prevent you from focusing fully on Allah (swt).

Conclusion

The actions and state of mind of a believer after completion of the prayer reflects the mood of the prayer itself. If the mind was pre-occupied with obstructive thoughts and worries during the prayer and no real connection to Allah (swt) occurred, then at the completion of the salām, the prayer mat would be folded and put away so that the activities of the day could continue. However, if the prayer was recited with concentration and connection, then, on the completion of the salām, the conversation with Allah (swt) would continue, the heart would be at rest and the day would unfold quite differently. If you realise that your concentration was wavering during the prayer, some methods have been suggested in this chapter that may help you regain focus for the next prayer.

Endnotes

1. al-Qumi, Mafatih al-Jinan, p.40.
2. al-Qumi, Mafatih al-Jinan, p.41.
3. First the right cheek and then the left cheek.
4. al-Kulaynī, *al-Kāfī*, vol. 2, p. 98.
5. al-Ṣadūq, *'Ilāl al-Sharāyi'*, vol. 2, p. 360.
6. Ibn Ḥanbal, *Musnad 'Aḥmad b. Ḥanbal*, vol. 5, p. 153.

Chapter 6: The Spiritual Upliftment

Building an accurate and positive mindset to prayer is essential for greater spiritual upliftment. Eighteen valuable suggestions that can holistically improve concentration are presented below.

In this chapter:

73. Worship Allah (swt) as if you see Him
74. Remember death
75. Pray on time
76. Divide the time between the ẓuhr and 'aṣr prayers and maghrib and 'ishā' prayers
77. Use your prayer time to find inner peace
78. Have hope in Allah and believe that He will accept your prayer
79. Do not worship Allah out of fear but worship Him as He is worthy of worship
80. Remember when you were at the peak of your spirituality
81. Ask Allah (swt) in your du'ā to help you concentrate in prayer
82. Pray at a mosque or an Islamic centre
83. Attempt to vary your place of prayer

84. Pray the nawāfil as it compensates for the lack of concentration in prayer
85. Give importance to night prayers
86. Pray congregational prayers
87. Divide your time between fajr prayer and sunrise
88. Plan your work around prayer and not prayer around work
89. Exhibit nervousness, shame and guilt before Allah (swt) over your sins
90. Focus on the 'eternal now'

73- Worship Allah (swt) as if you see Him

Some of us lose concentration in prayer because prayer has become a conversation with the self rather than with Allah (swt). For the conversation with the Almighty to take place, we need to worship Him as if we see Him and by truly believing in the unseen. This can only happen through having an attentive heart. Imam Khomeini (ra) said in this regard: *"All the ears of his heart will be closed to all other creatures, while the eye of his insight opens to the pure Beauty of the Lord of Majesty, discerning nothing else."*[1]

To be able to see Him, we truly believe that Allah (swt) is looking at us as we stand in prayer, and that the angels surround us at every single movement, witnessing our actions. If we do not make an effort to open our heart to Allah (swt), we are losing the opportunity to get close to Him. In that case, we should say in our heart: *"Shame on me! the Almighty is looking at me and is inviting me for a conversation with Him and I give Him a blind eye and a closed heart! O Allah, help me open the eye of my insight to your Majesty."*

It is narrated that Imām al-Bāqir (as) has quoted the Holy Prophet (saw) as saying:

إذا قام العبد المؤمن في صلاته نظر الله عزّ وجلّ إليه ، أو قال : أقبل الله عليه حتى ينصرف ، وأظلّته الرحمة ، من فوق رأسه إلى أُفق السماء ، والملائكة تحفّه من حوله إلى أُفق السماء ، ووكّل الله به ملكاً قائماً على رأسه يقول له : أيّها المصلّي ، لو تعلم من ينظر إليك ومن تناجي ما التفتّ ولا زلت من موضعك أبداً

"When a believing servant stands for the prayer, Allah, the Exalted, looks at him [or he said: He turns to him] until he finishes; Mercy shades him from above, the angels surround him from all sides, up to the horizon of the heaven, and Allah assigns an angel to stand at his head, saying: 'O praying one, if only you knew who is looking at you, and to whom you are supplicating, you would not look sideways at anything else, and nor would you leave your position.'"[2]

74- Remember death

To communicate with Allah (swt) during prayer with a soft and present heart, it is recommended to constantly be mindful of death. It is narrated from the Prophet (saw):

رسول الله صلى الله عليه وآله :أكثروا من ذكر هادم اللذات، فقيل: يا

رسول الله فما هادم اللذات؟ قال:الموت

"The Messenger of Alah said: 'Remember often the destroyer of pleasures.' They asked, 'What is the destroyer of pleasures, O Prophet of Allah?' He replied, 'Death.'"[3]

The faculty of imagination is powerful and this can be utilised for one's own benefit. Imagine you have reached the end of your life and your time in this life is over. Imagine your loneliness in the grave and the questioning of the angels Munkar and Nakīr. Bear in mind that your prayer will be with you in the grave testifying as to its validity during your lifetime.

Pondering on the inevitability of death will surely fill one's heart with fear and humility. This is best described in Du'ā' 'Abū Ḥamzah al-Thumālī:

وَارْحَمْنِي صَرِيعاً عَلَى الْفِرَاشِ تُقَلِّبُنِي أَيْدِي أَحِبَّتِي وَتَفَضَّلْ عَلَيَّ مَمْدُوداً

عَلَى الْمُغْتَسَلِ يُقَلِّبُنِي صَالِحُ جِيرَتِي وَتَحَنَّنْ عَلَيَّ مَحْمُولاً قَدْ تَنَاوَلَ الأَقْرِبَاءُ

أَطْرَافَ جِنَازَتِي وَجُدْ عَلَيَّ مَنْقُولاً قَدْ نَزَلْتُ بِكَ وَحِيداً فِي حُفْرَتِي وَارْحَمْ فِي

ذَلِكَ الْبَيْتِ الْجَدِيدِ غُرْبَتِي حَتَّى لا أَسْتَأْنِسَ بِغَيْرِكَ

"Confer Your benevolence on me when I am (laying) motionless on the (death) bed so that the beloved of my relatives surround me, and grant me Your bountifulness when I am stretched on the funeral bath so that the good-deeded of my community may wash me, and bestow Your kindred tenderness upon me when

I am carried while my relatives hand over the extremities of my coffin, and award me Your generosity when I am transported and finally delivered and left alone in my grave, and have mercy on my solitary confinement in this new residence so that I may not be comforted by anyone but You."[4]

One of the best ways to remember death is to frequently remember your peers, relatives, and friends who have passed away. Remember their deaths, their funerals, and their bodies beneath the ground. Remember what they used to look like, the positions they held, and how they lived their lives – and how their bodies are now within the grave, their spouses widowed, their children orphaned, their wealth lost and their positions filled by others. When you have considered each one of their lives, think about your life and consider yourself to be one of them and that the time will also come when people will remember you.

75- Pray on time

We learn from the traditions of the Holy Prophet (saw) and the Ahl al-Bayt (as) that they disconnected from people and their affairs at the time of prayer and focused on supplication and privacy with the Absolute Perfect One (swt).

We are all aware that when it is the time for prayer we must leave all worldly things and approach prayer. However, being aware is one thing and actually applying it is another. When the call for prayer comes and Allah is requesting His servant to meet Him, do we respond to this call or not?

إِنَّ الصَّلَاةَ كَانَتْ عَلَى الْمُؤْمِنِينَ كِتَابًا مَّوْقُوتًا

The prayer is indeed a timed prescription for the faithful. (4:103)

One might question why prayer is enjoined on believers at stated times. There are several possible reasons for this. Firstly, one of the fundamental purposes of prayer is remembrance. The five obligatory prayers are spread throughout the day, so we remember Allah in the morning, afternoon and the evening. Secondly, prayer is the 'meeting time' with our Lord when we spend uninterrupted time communicating with Him. Allah (swt) has set times for these meetings. If you had a meeting with a colleague at work or a friend, would you like to be late? And were this meeting to be with Allah (swt), surely we would want to be on time for the most important of all meetings. Having specific times for our prayers helps us manage our time for the day as it provides an order and a structure to our day. Furthermore, this is fundamental for concentration. Experts say that organising and structuring your day helps you concentrate on the tasks at hand, and this also applies to prayer.

To emphasise the importance of praying on time, it is narrared from Imām al-Ṣādiq (as) that he said:

من صلى الصلوات المفروضات في أوَّل وقتها فأقام حدودها ، رفعها الملك إلى السماء بيضاء نقية وهي تهتف به : حفظك الله كما حفظتني ، استودعك الله كما استودعتني ملَكاً كريماً ، ومن صلاَّها بعد وقتها من غير علّة فلم يُقم حدودها ، رفعها الملك سوداء مظلمة ، وهي تهتف به ضيعتني ضيعك الله كما ضيعتني ، ولا رعاك الله كما لم ترعني

"When someone offers an obligatory ṣalāt at the beginning of its time and observes its prerequisites, an angel takes it up to the heaven, white and pure, whereby it (i.e. the ṣalāt) says, 'May God take care of you as you took care of me. I have been delivered into the custody of a noble angel.' But when someone offers it after its time has elapsed, without any excuse, and does not observe its pre-requisite etiquette, it is taken up by an angel, black and dark, while it calls out to him (i.e. the one who offered the prayer), 'You neglected me. May God neglect you in the same manner that you neglected me. May God not take care of you in the same way that you did not take care of me.'"[5]

Women in their menstruation period can also worship Allah (swt) at the time of prayer. The daily prayers are an opportunity to dedicate a specific time to worship and remember Allah (swt) during the day and this can still be maintained while a woman is in her menstruation period. She can sit in her place of prayer, facing the qiblah, recite ṣalawāt, du'ā' and contemplate on the creation of Allah (swt). Through this, she can continue to be in the vicinity of the Almighty five times a day, even during her menstruation.

76-Divide the time between the zuhr and 'asr and maghrib and 'isha' prayers

Many people routinely combine ẓuhr and 'aṣr prayers and maghrib and 'ishā' prayers and not pray them at their respected times. It is permissible to separate the prayers and in fact, some scholars recommend separating the prayers. There are three main reasons for this:

a) It gives the believer the opportunity to come back to Allah (swt) more frequently as the prayers are more spread throughout during the day.

b) It can serve as a 'shock to the system' by changing what is usually a routine personal prayer timetable.

c) It gives the believer more time to prepare for the next prayer as some may find it difficult to concentrate for two consecutive prayers.

In some circumstances it is difficult to separate the prayers (for example, while at work or travelling), but one can attempt to pray each prayer at their respected time when they are able to do so.

77- Use your prayer time to find inner peace

Although grief can sometimes be considered as a helpful emotion for concentration in prayer, feeling down with great sadness or even with depression resulting from worldly issues can create the opposite effect. With the stormy sea of life, many people have problems or calamities, ranging from death in the family, to an illness and other social and family related problems. In such circumstances, the believer may search for inner peace by strengthening his faith in Allah, through His remembrance, contemplating on the verses of the Holy Qur'ān, seeking patience, and recognising and believing that Allah (swt) knows his problems. If your calamity persists, remember the calamities that the prophets and the Imāms of the Ahl al-Bayt (as) went through and how they overcame these calamities with faith and perseverance. Remember that the only worry that we should have in our life is of lack of faith and the failure to fulfil the duties to Allah.

In short, find that inner peace by having faith and hope in Allah (swt), who is always close to us, knows us best and knows what is in our hearts.

78- Have hope in Allah and believe that He will accept your prayer

Hope comes from recognising Allah's mercy and kindness, and acknowledging His subtle plan. There is no sense in approaching prayer whilst thinking that Allah (swt) will not accept your prayer. If the prayer is performed with sincere intentions and an effort is made to concentrate and attain a state of submission in prayer, then one must believe that Allah (swt) will accept that prayer. It is narrated from Imām al-Riḍhā (as):

أحسن الظن بالله فإن الله عز وجل يقول:أنا عند حسن ظن عبدي المؤمن

بي إن خيراً فخير وإن شراً فشر

"Entertain the best opinion of Allah, for Allah says: I am as My servant thinks of Me, if good then that's what he experiences, and if bad then likewise."[6]

79- Do not worship Allah out of fear but worship Him as He is worthy of worship

Some perform the obligatory prayers because they fear Allah's (swt) punishment and divine wrath. Although arguably this is not wrong, it should not be the intention of the submissive believer. This is eloquently described by the Commander of the Faithful (as) in the following narration:

إلهي ما عبدتك خوفا من نارك، ولا طمعا في جنتك، ولكن وجدتك أهلا للعبادة فعبدتك

"My God, I do not worship You for the fear of Your Hell, nor for desire for Your Paradise. Rather, I have found You worthy of worship and so I worship You."[7]

Imām ʿAlī (as) in this narration does not imply that he does not fear Allah's punishment, nor does he not desire His Paradise, rather he believed that there was a more powerful and justifiable reason to worship Allah (swt): because Allah is worthy of being worshipped. His heart was immersed in the love of the Almighty that even if Allah was to send him to Hell, he would inform the inmates of Hell of his immense love for Allah (swt) (as narrated in Duʿā' 'Abū Ḥamzah al-Thumālī). The people who worship Allah (swt) out of gratitude and love for him are those who are free from any sins, and from Allah's punishment and wrath:

اِنَّ قوماً عَبْدوا اللهَ رَغْبَةً فَتِلْك عِبادَةُ التُّجارِ وَ اِنَّ قوماً عَبْدوا اللهَ رَهْبَةً فَتِلك عِبادَةُ الْعَبيدِ وَ اِنَّ قوماً اللهَ عَبْدوا شُكْراً فَتِلكَ عِبادَةُ الاَحْرارِ

"There is a group that worships Allah for gain; that is the worship of the trader and there is a group that worships Allah out of fear; that is the worship of the slave and there is a group that worships Allah out of gratitude; that is the worship of the free."[8]

80- Remember when you were at the peak of your spirituality

Humans can be weak and forgetful. Our 'levels' of spirituality might fluctuate in our lifetime, depending on our circumstances. To gain spirituality in prayer, it might be helpful to remember the peak of our spirituality; for instance, during the time of ḥajj or 'umrah pilgrimage, a zīyārah or a significant life event. Remembering the sweetness of those spiritual days might help attain spirituality in prayer.

81- Ask Allah (swt) in your du'a to help you concentrate in prayer

Allah (swt) loves those who strive hard in His way, so revert to Allah (swt) and ask Him to help you concentrate in prayer, as Prophet Ibrāhīm (as) did:

Du'ā' for Concentration

رَبِّ اجْعَلْنِي مُقِيمَ الصَّلَاةِ وَمِنْ ذُرِّيَّتِي ۚ رَبَّنَا وَتَقَبَّلْ دُعَاءِ

My Lord! Make me a maintainer of the prayer,
and my descendants [too].
Our Lord, accept my supplication. (14:40)

Of course action is also needed with sincere du'ā' if one is to sustain concentration in prayer. This also includes continuous attempts and efforts and not to despair and give up on Allah's help and mercy as Prophet Ya'qūb (as) informed his sons when he requested them to look for Prophet Yūsuf (as) and his brother:

يَا بَنِيَّ اذْهَبُوا فَتَحَسَّسُوا مِنْ يُوسُفَ وَأَخِيهِ وَلَا تَيْأَسُوا مِنْ رَوْحِ اللَّهِ ۖ إِنَّهُ
لَا يَيْأَسُ مِنْ رَوْحِ اللَّهِ إِلَّا الْقَوْمُ الْكَافِرُونَ

O my sons! Go and inquire respecting Yūsuf and his brother, and despair not of Allah's mercy; surely none despairs of Allah's mercy except the unbelieving people. (12:87)

Furthermore, concentration in prayer must be achieved naturally without feeling the pressure to concentrate. In any Islamic action, the believer must seek to try their utmost to perform the action. This is all that is expected:

وَأَنْ لَيْسَ لِلْإِنْسَانِ إِلَّا مَا سَعَىٰ وَأَنَّ سَعْيَهُ سَوْفَ يُرَىٰ

And that nothing belongs to man except what he strives for, and that he will soon be shown his endeavour. (53:39-40)

Exercising the heart and mind to concentrate fully in prayer will in no doubt be difficult, but Allah (swt) has guaranteed us success after difficulty, as stated by these two verses:

فَإِنَّ مَعَ الْعُسْرِ يُسْرًا

إِنَّ مَعَ الْعُسْرِ يُسْرًا

Indeed ease accompanies hardship. Indeed ease accompanies hardship. (94:5-6)

82- Pray at a mosque or an Islamic centre

Whenever possible, attempt to pray your prayer in a mosque or prayer hall. Standing in a house of Allah (swt) and in front of Him (swt) can help you increase your attention in your prayers:

قُلْ أَمَرَ رَبِّي بِالْقِسْطِ ۖ وَأَقِيمُوا وُجُوهَكُمْ عِنْدَ كُلِّ مَسْجِدٍ وَادْعُوهُ مُخْلِصِينَ لَهُ الدِّينَ ۚ كَمَا بَدَأَكُمْ تَعُودُونَ

Say, 'My Lord has enjoined justice,' and [He has enjoined,] Set your heart [on Him] at every masjid [or every occasion of prayer], and invoke Him, putting your exclusive faith in Him. Even as He brought you forth in the beginning, so will you return. (7:29)

It is also narrated from Imām al-Ṣādiq (as) that he said:

عليكم باتيان المساجد، فإنها بيوت الله في الأرض، ومن أتاها متطهرا طهره الله من ذنوبه، وكتب من زواره

"I request you to attend the mosques, for they are houses of Allah (swt) on earth, and whoever enters it with purity, Allah will purify him from his sins, and he will be written from His visitors."[9]

If the mosque or the place of prayer is decorated with the verses of the Holy Qur'ān and the names of Allah (swt), one may feel the spiritual strength the environment provides while he is uttering the words of the Holy Qur'ān during prayer. Furthermore, the mosque or the place of worship usually symbolises peace and tranquillity; two essential ingredients for concentration in prayer. And finally, the mosque provides the opportunity for congregational prayers, which symbolise the unity and strength of Muslims (see point 86).

Attendance to mosques has been declining all around the world.[10] For example, a poll conducted in the United

Kingdom showed 48% of Muslims in the UK have never attended a mosque and 6% said they only attend for special occasions.[11] This disappointing statistic contributes to the lack of connection with our prayer observed by many of us. Also, a mosque is not just for worship, it serves other purposes, such as a place for learning and social gathering.

On a different but related note, Sir William Muir writes in his book, *The Life of Muhammad*, about the Prophet Muḥammad's (saw) activities in the Holy Mosque in Madina:

> "Though crude in material, and insignificant in dimensions, the Mosque of Muhammad is glorious in the history of Islam. Here, the Prophet and his companions spent most of their time; here, the daily service, with its oft-recurring prayers was first publicly established; and here, the great congregation assembled every Friday, listening with reverence and awe to messages from Heaven. Here, the Prophet planned his victories; here he received embassies from vanquished and contrite tribes; and from hence issued edicts, which struck terror amongst the rebellious to the very outskirts of the peninsula."[12]

83- Attempt to vary your place of prayer

There are some that prefer to pray in an allocated prayer room (see point 18). However others have reported that their concentration in prayer has improved when they pray in different places; be it at different rooms in their residence or in a different location. There are several reasons why this can be beneficial:

a. If you have the opportunity then attempt to pray in the open surrounded by nature (such as your garden) witnessing the limitless signs of Allah (swt). It could also be useful to travel if possible to the wilderness or near a waterfall for example to feel the calmness of nature and observe and contemplate on the wonderful creations of Allah (swt) in preparation for prayer and worship.

b. The Earth will bear witness in the Hereafter for the person's actions in this world. Therefore, praying at multiple places can serve as a witness to you in the next world as narrated by the Imām al-Ṣādiq (as):

صلوا من المساجد في بقاع مختلفة فإن كل بقعة تشهد للمصلي عليها يوم القيامة

"Pray in mosques at different spots (on this earth) as every spot will bear witness to the person who prayed on the Day of Judgment."[13]

84- Pray the nawafil as it compensates for the lack of concentration in prayer

Nawāfil, or supererogatory prayers, are optional recommended prayers a believer can pray that have abundant rewards. Since these prayers are additions to the obligatory prayers, they are called nawāfil (singular nāfilah), which means 'surplus' in Arabic. There are many narrations that state the importance of praying the nawāfil and some are noted below:

a. Getting closer to Allah (swt) and loving Him as narrated from ḥadīth al-qudsī from the Holy Prophet (saw):

ما تقرب إلي عبد بشئ أحب إلي مما افترضت عليه، وإنه ليتقرب إلي بالنافلة حتى أحبه، فإذا أحببته كنت سمعه الذي يسمع به، وبصره الذي يبصر به، ولسانه الذي ينطق به، ويده التي يبطش بها، إن دعاني أجبته، وإن سألني أعطيته

"My servant does not draw near to Me with anything better than his doing that which I have enjoined upon him, and My servant keeps drawing near to Me by doing nawāfil (supererogatory) prayers until I love him. And when I love him, I am his hearing with which he hears, his vision with which he sees, his tongue with which he speaks, his hand with which he strikes and his foot with which he walks. Were he to ask Me for anything, I would give it to him, if he were to call on Me, I would respond." [14]

b. Compensation for lack of concentration. It is narrated from Imām al-Bāqir (as) that he said:

إنما جعلت النافلة ليتم بها ما يفسد من الفريضة.

"Verily the supererogatory acts (nāfilah) of worship have been laid down in order to compensate for that which is vitiated out of the obligatory acts."[15]

It is narrated that Imām al-Ṣādiq (as) said:

يرفع للرجل من الصلاة ربعها أو ثمنها أو نصفها أو أكثر بقدر ما سها

ولكن الله تعالى يتم ذلك بالنوافل

"Out of the prayers offered by a man only a half of it or one-fourth or one-eighth rises to heaven in accordance with the extent of his lapses therein. However, God the Exalted, compensates for it by means of the supererogatory prayers."[16]

The nawāfil prayers are 34 rak'at, double the number of the obligatory prayers. They are as follows:

Fajr nāfilah: two rak'ah to be performed before the obligatory prayer;

Ẓuhr nāfilah: eight rak'ah (prayed two rak'at at a time) to be performed before the obligatory prayer

'Aṣr nāfilah: eight rak'ah (prayed two rak'at at a time) to be performed before the obligatory prayer

Maghrib nāfilah: four rak'ah (prayed two rak'at at a time) to be performed after the obligatory prayer

'Ishā' nāfilah: two rak'ah prayed while in the sitting position, (counted as one) to be performed after the obligatory prayer

Layl nāfilah: eight rak'at, prayed two at a time, to be performed before the fajr prayer

Shafā'ah nāfilah: two rak'at, to be performed after layl nāfilah and before fajr prayer

Witr nāfilah: one rak'at, to be performed after shafā'ah nāfilah and before fajr prayer.

Some jurisprudential rulings of obligatory prayers have been wavered for nawāfil prayers.[17] For example, you only need to recite sūrah al-Fātiḥah before proceeding to rukū'; you may pray the nawāfil while sitting or standing (standing is better) or even in a car; and if you make mistakes you do not need to do sajdah al-sahw.[18] This ease is to encourage the believers to pray the nawāfil so as to gain its many benefits and rewards.

85-Give importance to night prayers

It is recommended to pray all nawāfil prayers, but special emphasis is given to the night prayers (layl, shafā'ah and witr nāfilah; also known as tahajjud prayers).[19] It was obligatory on the Holy Prophet (saw) to spend part of the night in worship[20] and performing the night prayers:

وَمِنَ اللَّيْلِ فَتَهَجَّدْ بِهِ نَافِلَةً لَكَ عَسَىٰ أَنْ يَبْعَثَكَ رَبُّكَ مَقَامًا مَحْمُودًا

And keep vigil for a part of the night, as a superogatory [devotion] for you It may be that your Lord will raise you to a praised position. (17:79)

True believers follow the Prophet's path by waking up at night and worshipping Allah when others are asleep. It is a time where one can find peace and tranquillity in Allah's presence. Night prayers are the honour of a believer, as narrated in the following ḥādīth from Imām al-Ṣādiq (as):

شرف المؤمن صلاة الليل وعز المؤمن كفه عن الناس

"The believer's honour is night prayers and his glory is refraining from (harming) people."[21]

Therefore, to increase spirituality and achieve the presence of Allah (swt) in your heart during prayer, attempt to perform the night prayers, even if it is only shafā'ah and witr prayers.

86- Pray congregational prayers

It is highly recommended to pray in congregation or jamāʿah. This ultimately builds a bond of togetherness and unity, and instils humility within the prayer. Allah (swt) says in the Holy Qurʾān:

وَأَقِيمُوا الصَّلَاةَ وَآتُوا الزَّكَاةَ وَارْكَعُوا مَعَ الرَّاكِعِينَ

And maintain the prayer, and give the zakāt, and bow along with those who bow [in prayer]. (2:43)

The word 'rākiʿīn' here is plural as it indicates that you should bow your head in worship in congregation with those who bow.

Many narrations note the importance of praying in congregation. For example, it is narrated from Zurārah that he asked Imām al-Ṣādiq (as):

عن زرارة قال، قلت لأبي عبد الله عليه السلام: ما يروي الناس أن الصلاة في جماعة أفضل من صلاة الرجل وحده بخمس وعشرين صلاة فقال: " صدقوا " فقلت: الرجلان يكونان جماعة؟ فقال: " نعم، ويقوم الرجل عن يمين الإمام "

"People narrate prayer in congregation is greater than 25 years of a single person's prayer? The Imām said: Believe this. I said: What about two people praying in congregation? He said: Yes, and the man should pray on the right of the imām."[22]

Such emphasis on congregational prayer must mean that it has many benefits and strengths. In addition to providing strength of unity and togetherness, it also provides spiritual nourishment. When we are in congregation, we feel the spiritual warmth inside the room; one may not know the person beside him, but he knows that he is in the same place as himself, seeking to communicate with his Lord and submit to His Majesty. This is one of the reasons why at the end of the prayer, people sitting adjacent to each other exchange handshakes and supplicate to Allah (swt) for the acceptance of each other's prayers.

Congregational prayers are recommended anywhere and with as little as two people.[23] Families and friends should try to make it a habit to pray in congregation whenever it is possible to make use of the benefits it provides them.

Furthermore, to stay focused during the ẓuhr and ʿaṣr congregational prayers whilst the imām is standing and reciting quietly, it is recommended to softly recite some tasbīḥ, such as *"Subḥān 'Allāh"*; *"Glory be to Allah"*, *"Al-ḥamdu li 'Allāh"*; *"Praise be to Allah"*, *"Astaghfir Allāh"*; *"I seek forgiveness from Allah"*. The tasbīḥ serves not only to keep us focused, but also to keep us in the remembrance and in the vicinity of Allah (swt) during the congregation.

87-Divide your time between fajr and sunrise

It is highly recommended to spend the time between fajr prayers and sunrise with absolute contemplation and worship of Allah (swt). It is the time when the believer is unlikely to be engaged in work or other activities, thus having the opportunity to spend the time in worship. Sayyid 'Abd al-Ḥusayn Dastghayb in his book, *Prayer of a Submissive Believer*, suggests dividing the time between fajr and sunrise to perform the following acts of worship:[24]

1. To remember Allah (swt) and perform various tasbīḥ; in praticular the tasbīḥāt al-Zahrā (as).

2. To read the du'ā' recommended for that particular time of day.

3. To read the Holy Qur'ān.

4. To mention your sins; ask Allah (swt) for forgiveness; and promise Allah that you will not commit those sins again.

Together with spending time in worship prior to sunrise, the Holy Qur'ān advises us to do the same prior to sunset, during the night and during the day:

فَاصْبِرْ عَلَىٰ مَا يَقُولُونَ وَسَبِّحْ بِحَمْدِ رَبِّكَ قَبْلَ طُلُوعِ الشَّمْسِ وَقَبْلَ غُرُوبِهَا ۖ وَمِنْ آنَاءِ اللَّيْلِ فَسَبِّحْ وَأَطْرَافَ النَّهَارِ لَعَلَّكَ تَرْضَىٰ

So be patient with what they say, and celebrate the praise of your Lord before the rising of the sun and before the sunset, and glorify Him in watches of the night and at the day's ends, that you may be pleased. (20:130)

88- Plan your work around prayer and not prayer around work

It might be considered as a luxury to be able to plan work around prayer times, especially if the nature of the work does not allow for this. However, try to do this whenever possible. When arranging meetings, appointments, and lunch dates, be wary of the prayer time and be prepared (have a compass, a prayer mat, and be in wuḍū) for the prayer. Instil in your mind when you wake up in the morning that nothing is more important on this day than prayers as no meeting or work is more important than the meeting with the Almighty. By doing so, you have planned for prayer to be performed on time.

89- Exhibit nervousness, shame and guilt before Allah (swt) over your sins

Imagine you are standing in front of the Almighty in the Hereafter. How would you be feeling? Surely feelings of nervousness, shame and guilt would be evident due to the numerous sins that one has committed in his life.

Awakening a sense of nervousness, shamefulness or guilt undoubtedly revolutionises the soul in a believer. The heart melts with fear and awe as the believer senses his personal shortcomings over the sins that he has committed in his life. An innate sense of modesty also becomes an internal restraint to the believer, which helps him maintain the correct 'akhlāq and values. All this is encompassed in the umbrella of faith ('īmān) as narrated by Imām al-Ṣādiq (as):

الحياء من الايمان والايمان في الجنة

"Modesty is from faith ('īmān), and whoever has faith will be granted Paradise."[25]

Furthermore, whilst in communication with Allah (swt), the feeling of genuine remorse as a result of the sins committed, or as a result of one's lack of concentration in the prayers helps to bring the heart closer to Allah (swt) and establish the presence of the heart during the prayer. It also helps while one is in that state of modesty, shame and guilt to mention one's sins after the prayer and shed some tears while asking Allah (swt) for forgiveness.

90- Focus on the 'eternal now'

Distracting thoughts are usually a result of an incident that has happened in the past or a situation that might occur in the future. Eckhart Tolle, the spiritual author, says in his book, *The Power of Now*, that we can never experience the past or the future, and the only thing that ever has any real value is the present or, what he calls, the 'eternal now'. He says:

> "You can always cope with the now, but you can never cope with the future - nor do you have to. The answer, the strength, the right action or the resource will be there when you need it, not before, not after."[26]

One of the biggest causes of lack of concentration in our prayers is the obstructive thoughts that appear randomly and at random stages of the prayer. If we begin to realise that these thoughts are related to the past or the future, and instead focus on the present prayer, we can turn our minds back to focusing on the communication with the Almighty during the prayer. This, of course, can be applied not just during prayer but before and after it too, as we set our minds to focus on the 'now' and ignore the worries that are usually a result of the past or the future.

Conclusion

Concentration in prayer cannot be achieved without applying continuous methods for spiritual upliftment, as man is constantly in need of strengthening the heart. In this chapter, general practical points have been suggested to increase the level of spirituality, such as praying on time, finding the inner peace, praying in congregation and exhibiting a sense of shame and guilt over one's sins. We ask Allah (swt) to help us in our journey towards strengthening our spirituality in order to attain His pleasure and reward, 'inshā Allāh.

Endnotes

1. Khomeini, *'Ādāb al-Ṣalāt: The Disciplines of the Prayer,* Discourse one, Chapter 9.
2. al-Kulaynī, *al-Kāfī*, vol. 3, p. 265.
3. al-Majlisī, *Biḥār Al-Anwār*, vol. 79, p.167.
4. Du'ā' 'Abū Ḥamzah al-Thumālī is a Du'ā' narrated by Imām 'Alī (as). It can be found in many du'ā' books and online: [http://www.duas.org/thumali.htm.] 18/03/2014. Translation of du'ā' taken from this website.
5. al-Ṣadūq, *al-'Amālī*, p. 328.
6. al-Kulaynī, *al-Kāfī*, vol. 2, p. 72.
7. al-Majlisī, *Biḥār Al-Anwār*, vol. 7, p.186.
8. al-Sharīf al-Raḍī, *Nahj al-Balāghah*, Wisdom (ḥikam) 238, p. 293 .
9. al-Ṣadūq, *al-'Amālī*, p. 440.
10. See [http://wikiislam.net/wiki/Muslim_Statistics_-_Mosques] 18/03/2014.
11. Anthony Wells - NOP Poll of British Muslims - UK Polling Report, August 8, 2006.
12. Muir, W. *The Life of Muhammed*, p. 177.

13. al-Ṣadūq, *al-'Amālī*, p. 440.
14. al-Kulaynī, *al-Kāfi*, vol. 2, p. 352.
15. al-Ṣadūq, *'Ilāl al-Sharāyi'*, vol. 2, p. 329.
16. al-Tūsī, *Tahdhīb al-'Aḥkām*, vol. 2, p. 341.
17. Yazdi, M. Comments by al-Sistānī. A. *al-Urwatul Withqa*. Part Two. p. 361-362.
18. These are two prostrations of forgetfulness. For information into how to perform this, refer to the books of jurisprudence.
19. All three known as ṣalātul layl, or night prayers.
20. Including performing the night prayers.
21. al-Ṣadūq, *Thawaab Al-a'amal,* p. 41.
22. al-Kulaynī, *al-Kāfi*, vol. 3, p. 371.
23. The jurisprudential rulings need to be considered here.
24. Dastghayb, *Ṣalāt al-Khāshi'iyn: Prayer of a Submissive Believer*, p. 64.
25. al-Kulaynī, *al-Kāfi*, vol. 2, p. 106.
26. E. Tolle, *The Power of Now*, p. 85.

Chapter 7: The Medical and Physical Activities

Concentration is an art that can be enhanced by certain techniques that have been physically and medically researched. Both body and soul should be fully present during prayer. The following are some of these techniques that one can use to increase their concentration in general.

In this chapter:

91. Eat a well balanced diet and exercise regularly
92. Have adequate sleep
93. Stay hydrated
94. Learn ways to meditate
95. Master stress management
96. Fast, or reduce your daily food intake
97. Sit still for a few minutes to increase your ability to concentrate
98. Gaze your eyes into a black spot
99. Improve your memory
100. Improve your posture

91- Eat a well balanced diet and exercise regularly

If we are serious about concentrating in our prayer, then we should also be serious about making sure our bodies and minds are in good shape. We cannot expect to sustain concentration in prayer if we eat unhealthily and do not exercise regularly. The body will become sluggish, which leads to a sluggish mind that will struggle to focus. The sluggish body will always feel tired and the brain will have a low attention span. It is therefore highly recommended to eat a well balanced diet and exercise as much as possible.

Harriet Griffey in *The Art of Concentration*, offers a different reason why exercise is important for concentration.[1] She states that sporting activities and exercise allow our body to do specific things that often involve coordination, balance and responsiveness so we have no choice but to really concentrate on what we are doing.

So let us make an effort to exercise regularly, not just to live longer, but with the intention of getting closer to Allah (swt). A thirty-minute walk every day will rejuvenate the body and mind, which will result in more focus and enthusiasm.

92- Have adequate sleep

Adequate sleep is absolutely essential for concentration. Studies show that sleep deprivation impairs endocrine and metabolic functions and thus affects concentration.[2] It is advisable to get sufficient sleep each night to keep you refreshed and focused. It is also recommended to sleep early if possible to be able to pray fajr prayer with a conscious mind. This, of course, also means that you can wake up early in the morning to begin your daily duties. Furthermore, it is recommended to take mid-day naps if possible, as the mufassirīn (the interpreters of the Holy Qur'ān) discuss the use of the power nap in the exegesis of this verse:

أَصْحَابُ الْجَنَّةِ يَوْمَئِذٍ خَيْرٌ مُسْتَقَرًّا وَأَحْسَنُ مَقِيلًا

On that day the inhabitants of Paradise will be in the best abode and an excellent resting place. (25:24)

Some exegeses[3] suggest that the word 'maqīla' here refers to a resting place at noon, also known as 'qaylūla'. To support this, recent studies show that power naps during the day can refresh the mind, increase alertness, productivity and improve memory and learning.[4] Other sleep-related acts which are recommended include performing wuḍū before sleep and sleeping on the right side (also known as the right lateral decubitus).

93- Stay hydrated

Dehydration, some researchers believe, is another reason for lack of concentration. They show that dehydration results in the possibility of experiencing fatigue and a decrease in mental agility.[5] It is therefore advised to stay hydrated which may clear the mind, reduces stress and leads to clearer thought. Allah (swt) describes water as living:

وَجَعَلْنَا مِنَ الْمَاءِ كُلَّ شَيْءٍ حَيٍّ ۖ أَفَلَا يُؤْمِنُونَ

And We made every living thing out of water, will they then not believe? (21:30)

To appreciate the deep meaning of this verse, imagine you are very thirsty on a hot day and are in desperate need of water; your body feels weak and dysfunctional. As you manage to sip some water, it is as if your soul has returned and you feel alive again. That is why the Qur'ān beautifully describes water as living.[6]

94- Learn ways to meditate

The core goal of meditation is to focus and eventually quieten the mind and free it from all obstructive thoughts. Meditation brings the mind to focus on one object, thus achieving strength of concentration.

Some techniques teach methods to relax the mind and achieve the accession to inner calm that is needed for concentration. One such technique is to breathe slowly and calmly.[7] You begin by sitting in a quiet and comfortable place. Close your eyes and focus on your breathing. Breathe in deeply and breathe out. Concentrate solely on your breathing, if a thought enters your mind; acknowledge it and clear your mind. The key here is to breathe from the abdomen and get as much oxygen in your lungs as possible. The higher levels of oxygen have a calming effect and relax the mind. Ten minutes of this exercise a day can channel concentration and help you master techniques to concentrate in prayer.

Another technique to help you relax your mind through breathing is to place one hand on your upper chest, the other on your abdomen. Breathe slowly allowing the abdominal muscles to move freely with the breath. Don't force or strain. The hand on the upper chest is there to remind you that the upper chest does not lift as you breathe in. Take several breaths in this way, allowing there to be a moment of full suspension of the in-breath before exhaling.[8]

If you are interested in other breathing techniques, you may like to research Equal Breathing, Alternate Nostril Breathing, and Progressive Relaxation.

95- Master stress management

The relationship between stress and concentration can be a negative one. Stress is not always bad; it can be useful for creativity and learning. However, stress only becomes harmful if it is overwhelming, as it disrupts the healthy state of the nervous system. This overwhelming stress can cause tiredness amongst many other symptoms and thus can reduce concentration.

If you believe that stress is one of the reasons why your mind wanders off during prayer then you should try some stress management techniques. One of these techniques is known as Progressive Muscular Relaxation (PMR), which was developed by a physician called Edmund Jacobson in the 1920s. His idea was simple: if you feel your muscles are tense, you should tense specific muscle groups and then relax them to create awareness of tension and relaxation. He proved that this technique could eventually lead to total muscle relaxation.[9]

Furthermore, some suggest hand massaging can relieve stress and headaches. The technique is massaging for around 90 seconds the web space of the hand that is between the thumb and forefinger.

96- Fast, or reduce your daily food intake

One of the reasons why fasting can increase concentration is that abstaining from food and drink breaks our routine lifestyle and habits, so we are more aware of what we are doing in our day, including the prayer. If you are used to approaching ẓuhr prayer after lunch then your brain will be more alert if that system is broken while fasting. Also, some people who fast experience their neediness for Allah (swt), which opens their heart to spiritual understanding. This can help the believer get closer to Allah (swt) in prayer.

Therefore, if you feel that fasting may increase your concentration and want to get extra reward from Allah (swt), then fasting may indeed be a viable option for you.

97- Sit still for a few minutes to increase your ability to concentrate

Harriet Griffey in her book, *The Art of Concentration*, explains how sitting still for a few minutes can help you stay calm, focused and increase your ability to concentrate in a task. She says:

> "Start by sitting in a relaxed position, upright in a chair, without slumping. Don't cross your legs; instead sit with you feet flat on the floor, your hands resting palms upwards on your thighs. Use your core muscles to support you, relax your shoulders, lengthen through the back of the neck and drop your chin a little. Try to breathe using your diaphragm and stomach muscles, not from the upper chest. Now sit still. Be aware of areas of discomfort but, having previously adjusted your position, don't move again; just register the thought and move on. Be aware

of any involuntary muscular movements, but consciously relax the limbs in which they occur, and move on. Stay concentrated on your body, rather than drifting away with your thoughts, and do this for five minutes. Don't extend the time, until you are really comfortable for five minutes."[10]

98- Gaze your eyes into a black spot

Fixing our eyes onto one particular space for a few moments can help to gain control over the involuntary muscular movements that may distract us from prayer. You can practise this outside of the prayer by gazing into a black spot in a wall about two inches in diameter. The trick is to consciously leave any thoughts to one side and get back to concentrating on the black spot. Do this for only three minutes a day and assess your concentration. If it is helping, then prolong this practice.

99- Improve your memory

All techniques used to improve memory involve concentration, as people are more likely to recall information which they concentrate on. Memory helps to direct attention to specific memorised events as it gives context for concentration. It is recommended therefore to memorise as many chapters of the Holy Qur'ān as possible and memorise the various supplications used in prayer (see point 45) that can improve concentration during prayer.

A recent study has shown a link between working memory and attention.[11] Matthew Cruger, a neuropsychologist, defines working memory as *"a set of skills that helps us keep information in mind while using that information to complete a task or execute a challenge".*[12] Others describe it as the brain's post-it note, or a mental workspace that allows you to juggle multiple thoughts simultaneously. The study showed that working memory may actually enable distractive thoughts (or what psychologists call task unrelated-thought) during a particular task (in our case prayer). They add,

> "What this study seems to suggest is that, when circumstances for the task aren't very difficult, people who have additional working memory resources deploy them to think about things other than what they're doing".[13]

They further suggest that if the task is complicated and difficult then the link between mind-wandering and working memory disappears.

Working memory is not a bad thing; many studies have in fact shown that it is needed to complete long tasks as described by Cruger: *"Working memory helps us stay involved in something longer and keep more things in mind while approaching a task."*[14] However, what we learn from the early study is that if our brain considers prayer as an uninteresting and very much routine task, then it will deploy working memory resources to occupy the mind with distractive thoughts that are 'more interesting' than the prayer. This is why we have to ensure that our prayer is not considered a systematic and a trivial task by alternating recitations and accomplishing the spiritual enhancements outlined in this book.

100- Improve your posture

It is important to be as comfortable as possible while praying. Having a poor posture and unnecessary levels of muscular and mental tension can lead to physical complications as well as reducing energy levels, which can have an impact on concentration. Maria Pattinson, a leadership and communication skills consultant, wrote some recommendations for a correct posture during prayer, exclusively for this book:

> "Posture is important in prayer because poor postural habits create aches and pains that can make it difficult to remain focused when praying. The daily wear and tear of sitting hunched over a desk or driving in heavy traffic or coping with the multitude of stresses that are part of contemporary life take their toll on our bodies. The result is felt as lower back problems, frozen shoulders, stiff necks, restricted breathing, painful joints – none of which are conducive to ease in the movements of Muslim prayer. If, on top of the aches and pains, we also start to feel annoyed or irritated with ourselves, then concentrated prayer seems to escape us even further. To help bring mind and body to a single focus in preparation for prayer, we would do well to draw upon the work of the Victorian reciter F.M. Alexander and his research into postural awareness known now as the Alexander Technique.
>
> F.M Alexander became aware, though his own vocal problems, that the human body responds to stimuli that are both internal and external. His observations about the use of his own self in the act of public speaking led him to the realization that the 'means whereby' one does an action is inextricably woven with the end that is gained.[15]

If we consider this comment in the light of the actions in praying, then perhaps it is worth considering that the 'means whereby' one becomes aware of posture in prayer will have an impact on the quality of prayer itself. Below is a sequence of actions to try out for yourself as a 'means whereby' during prayer which might bring the mind and body to the present moment, helping to leave the distractions of everyday life behind.

1. When you are in the standing position, stand with your weight equally balanced on two feet. Feel a sense of weight dropping down from the shoulders so that the lower part of the body is doing the supporting role. Check that knees are not locked back. Feel that the head is balanced lightly on top of the spinal column, floating up towards the ceiling, crown of the head the highest point, as if held up by a string from the crown of the head to the ceiling. Relax the jaws if they are tense.

2. Breathe through the nose and feel the breath reach down to the stomach. Let the out breath be longer than the in breath. Breathe and inspire yourself to a deeper sense of being present in your body. Breathe slowly, allowing the abdominal muscles to move freely with the breath. Don't force or strain. At the end of the out breath, wait for the natural impulse to take the next in breath. Do not hurry this moment or force the breath.

As you move through the various actions of the prayer, notice the effect on your breathing. Aim to keep the breathing low and flowing easily in the body as described above.

3. If your next action is doing rukūʿ or sujūd, be aware of unnecessary tensions; release them before actually progressing towards kneeling or prostrating.

By paying attention to the use of our bodies in prayer, we can learn to make less unnecessary effort and increase our capacity to open more fully to receive the blessings of Allah."

Conclusion

Islam is a holistic religion which not only guides us on how we should live our 'spiritual lives' but all facets of life as they are connected. In this chapter, a holistic approach to concentration has been presented. This is because the mind, body and soul embark on a journey during the prayer and so it is important to pay attention to all these faculties in order to maximise our concentration in prayer. If we eat a balanced diet, drink plenty of water, or trying different breathing techniques with the intention of improving concentration in prayer in order to connect to the Lord, then all these seemingly mundane acts become acts of worship, and actions fī sabīli Allāh, (for the sake of Allah). It is a beautiful way to remember Allah (swt) during the day and make our every action a step towards Him (swt).

Endnotes

1. H. Griffey, *The Art of Concentration*, p. 226.

2. Goel N, Rao H, Durmer JS, Dinges DF. Neurocognitive consequences of sleep deprivation. *Semin Neurol*. 2009; vol 29, p320–39.

3. al-Shirazi. *Al-'Amthāl fī Tafsīr al-Qur'ān,* vol. 11. p. 170.

4. C. E. Milner, K. A. Cote. Benefits of napping in healthy adults: impact of nap length, time of day, age, and experience with napping. *J Sleep Res*. 18(2): p. 272–281, 2009.

5. Ganio MS et. al (2011). Mild dehydration impairs cognitive performance and mood of men. *Br J Nutr*. vol 106, p.1535-43

6. al-Shirazi. *Al-'Amthāl fī Tafsīr al-Qur'ān,* vol. 10. p110

7. See [http://www.helpguide.org/mental/stress_relief_meditation_yoga_relaxation.htm] 18/03/2014.

8. Taken from [http://www.mindtools.com/pages/main/newMN_TCS.htm] 14/10/2013.

9. See [http://www.amsa.org/healingthehealer/musclerelaxation.cfm] 14/10/2013.

10. H. Griffey, *The Art of Concentration*, p. 196.

11. D. Levinson, J. Smallwood, R. Davidson. (2012) The Persistence of Thought: Evidence for a Role of Working Memory in the Maintenance of Task-Unrelated Thinking, *Psychol Sci*. vol. 23, p. 375–380.

12. See [http://www.ncld.org/types-learning-disabilities/executive-function-disorders/what-is-working-memory-why-does-matter] 16/10/2013.

13. D. Levinson, J. Smallwood, R. Davidson. (2012) The Persistence of Thought: Evidence for a Role of Working Memory in the Maintenance of Task-Unrelated Thinking, *Psychol Sci*. vol. 23, p. 375–380.

14. See [http://www.ncld.org/types-learning-disabilities/executive-function-disorders/what-is-working-memory-why-does-matter] 16/10/2013.

15. F.M.Alexander , *The Use of The Self*, p. 66-69.

Conclusion

101- Keep going and never give up

Sustaining concentration in prayer is a journey. It is not something that can be achieved in one day, especially if a person aims to concentrate in every prayer. Rather, it is an effort that must be exercised for every prayer, and it is only after a sustained effort that true results can be seen.

There will be times when the heart yearns for connection with the Almighty and concentration is natural and the conversation is sweet. There may be other times, when you are tired or not in the right state of mind to concentrate. You may face situations when you are busy with work and family and find it difficult to clear your mind for prayer. If these situations and feelings occur, do not give up as these situations are part of the struggle towards achieving submissiveness during prayer.

It is inevitable that there will be fluctuations in our quest to strengthen our concentration in prayer, as it is also the case for our faith and 'īmān in Allah (swt). The mark of a successful believer is to continuously strive and make an effort to strengthen faith in Allah (swt) and connection during prayer, even when faced with obstacles along the way. Through this, Allah (swt) will reward the believer, even though they may not have reached the level of concentration needed during prayer.

So persevere with the knowledge that Allah (swt) sees all your efforts. He has promised to be with the patient ones, and grant them a reward without measure as described in the Holy Qur'ān:

إِنَّمَا يُوَفَّى الصَّابِرُونَ أَجْرَهُمْ بِغَيْرِ حِسَابٍ

Those who patiently persevere will truly receive a reward without measure. (39:10)

This is not the end. This is the beginning of the journey towards achieving presence of the heart through a continual struggle against the Shayṭān and distracting thoughts during prayer. We pray to Allah (swt) to grant us the tawfīq to continue in the journey towards Him and to keep going and never give up.

In Summary

Prayer represents a concrete manifestation of obedience, patience, faith, servitude and freewill. Its essence is sincerity and humility towards the All-Encompassing and Merciful. It opens the heart and mind to Allah and purifies the heart from all filth and impurity. It is the act that if it is accepted, all other actions are accepted, and if it is rejected, all other actions are rejected. This means that the whole lifestyle and understanding of a person affects his prayer. It is like a sport, where to play well during a match, you need to practice regularly, live a healthy lifestyle and go running; or an exam where you need to have studied more than what is actually on the exam in order to pass it.

The Commander of the Faithful put it best when he said that worshippers are of three types.[1] The first are those who worship out of fear, and this is the worship of servants: there are plenty of reasons to fear lack of concentration in prayer, as there is no acceptance without concentration and presence of heart. If there is no acceptance of actions then how will we know we are safe on the Day of Judgment, even if we do fulfil the outward bounds of religion? We know of examples from history of tyrants who are cursed by Allah (swt) to an eternity in Hellfire, and are deprived of His Mercy, yet they also recited their obligatory prayers. It is narrated from Prophet Muḥammad (saw):

كَمْ مِنْ صَائِمٍ لَيْسَ لَهُ مِنْ صِيَامِهِ إِلاَّ الْجُوعُ وَ الظَّمَأُ، وَكَمْ مِنْ قَائِمٍ لَيْسَ لَهُ مِنْ قِيَامِهِ إِلاَّ السَّهَرُ وَ الْعَنَاءُ

"Many receive nothing from fasting except hunger and thirst, and many receive nothing from their prayers except vigil and weakness."[2]

The second group Imām ʿAlī (as) speaks about are those who worship for a reward, and this is the worship of the traders. To trade with Allah (swt), we must have something that is worth trading. If the basic requirement for prayer is concentration, then we must really question the true *value* of our prayer. You cannot trade something of low value for something of a very high value. It is true that Allah (swt) is Generous, but now there is much more to gain.

The third group of people are those who worship out of thankfulness, or because they realise that He deserves to be worshipped, and this is the worship of the freeman. The motivation for their worship is based on their knowledge of Allah (swt) and their understanding . They increase in their concentration with their increase in love and knowledge and their prayer really is a connection to Allah (swt). Every prayer they make moves them closer and closer. There comes a time when the world disappears when they stand on their prayer mat. Like Imām ʿAlī (as), himself, who is known as the Leader of the Pious and Those who Pray (Imām al-Mutaqīn wa al-Muṣallīn).

The Commander of the Faithful (as) was at the peak of this third group, and he shows us the possibilities that prayer can offer. However, we must all know that everyone has a potential to fulfil, and if we make a serious attempt to channel at least a tenth of our care for this world towards the Herefter we would certainly achieve some presence of the heart in prayer. Let us begin today by gradually striving towards this path and continuously practising the various methods needed to attain the pleasure of proximity to Allah (swt).

Endnotes

1. al-Sharīf al-Raḍī, *Nahj al-Balāghah*, Wisdom (ḥikam) 238, p. 293
2. al-Sharīf al-Raḍī, *Nahj al-Balāghah*, Wisdom (ḥikam) 145, p. 282

Bibliography

Al-ʿĀmilī Z. (al-Shahīd al-Thānī), *Rasāʾil al-Shahīd al-Thānī*, (Arabic). Qum, 2000.

Ahlul Bayt Digital Islamic Library Project Team, *A Shi'ite Encyclopedia*. Prayer (Ṣalāt): According to Five Islamic Schools of Law, Part 1. [http://www.al-islam.org/shiite-encyclopedia-ahlul-bayt-dilp-team] 02/02/2014.

Albani, M.N., *The Ṣalāh in the Light of the Prophet's Tradition*, Islamic Book Trust, Kuala Lumpur, 2005.

Al-Barqī, A., *al-Maḥāsin*, Corrections and Comments by al-Hussaini, J.D. (Arabic). Tehran, 1992.

Dastghayb, A.H., *Ṣalāt al-Khāshiʿiyn: Prayer of a Submissive Believer*. (Arabic). Dār al-Taʿāruf, Beirut, 1995.

Fadlullah, M.H., *Tafsīr Min Waḥy al-Qurʾān*. (Arabic). Dār al-Malik. Beirut, 1998.

Griffey, H., *The Art of Concentration*. Macmillan Publishers Limited. Oxford, 2010.

Hāʾirī, F., *Miṣbāḥ al-Sharīʿah: The Lantern of the Path*, Ansariyan Publications. Qum 2004.

Ibn Ḥanbal, A., *Musnad ʾAḥmad b. Ḥanbal*. (Arabic). [http://shiaonlinelibrary.com]. 10/02/2014

Isfahani, M.M., *Ṣalāt (Prayer): The Mode of Divine Proximity and Recognition*, [http://www.al-islam.org/salat-prayer-mode-divine-proximity-and-recognition-ayatullah-mirza-mahdi-isfahani,]. 19/10/2013

Al-Jawharī, *al-Ṣiḥāh al-Lughah Arabic Dictionary,* [http://www.baheth.info]. 08/01/2014

Kabbani, H., 'The Importance and Meaning of Prayer in Islam' in Cornell, V. (general ed.), '*Voices of Islam*', vol. 2, United States, 2007.

Kashani, M.F., *al-Mahajjah al-Bayḍā' fī Tahdhīb al-'Aḥyā'*, (Arabic). Intisharāt Islamī, Jāmi'a-yi Mudarrisīn, Qum, 1996.

Kermalli, J., *Concentration in Prayer,* Tabligh Centre. Tanzania, 2003.

Khomeini, R., *'Ādāb al-Ṣalāt: The Disciplines of the Prayer*, trans. M.J. Khalili, Second Revised Edition. The Institute for Compilation and Publication of Imam Khomeini's Works. [www.al-islam.org/adab], 6/11/2013.

Al-Kulaynī, M., *Uṣūl al-Kāfī*, (Arabic). Dār al-Kutub al-Islāmīya. Tehran, 2000.

Mahdavi, S. *Forty 'Aḥādīth on Ṣalāt*, Islamic Education Board of the World Federation of KSIMC, [http://www.al-islam.org/forty-ahadith-on-salat], 02/02/2014.

Al-Majlisī, M.B., *Biḥār Al-Anwār*, (Arabic). Mu'assisah al-Wafā'a, Beirut, 1983.

Ibn Manẓūr, *Lisān al-'Arab Dictionary,* [http://www.baheth.info]. 08/01/2014

McElwain, T., *The Secret Treasures of Salaat*, Minerva Press, London, 1997.

Mirzā, al-Nūrī, *Mustadrak al-Wasā'il*, Mu'assisah Āl al-Bayt li Iḥyā' al-Turāth. Beirut, 1988

Muir, W., *The Life of Muhammed*, Oliver and Boyd, Edinburgh, 1923.

Qara'i, 'A.Q., trans, *The Qur'ān, with a Phrase-by-Phrase English Translation*, ICAS Press, London, 2004.

Qarā'atī, M., *The Radiance of the Secrets of Prayer*, Ahlul Bayt World Assembly, Tehran, 2013.

Qarā'atī, M., *A Commentary on Prayer*, trans. M.L. Limba, Ahlul Bayt World Assembly, Tehran, 2011.

Qummī, A., *Mafātīḥ al-Jinān*, Dār al-Thawī, Al-Qurbā li al-Ṭab'ah wa al-Nashr, Qum, 2003.

Al-Raḍī, A.S., *Nahj al-Balāghah*, Ahlul Bayt Assembly of America, Maryland, 1996.

Sabziwari, *Jāmi' al-Akhbār*, (Arabic). Mu'assisah Āl al-Bayt li Iḥyā' al-Turāth. Qum, 1990.

Al-Ṣadūq, M.B.A., *Thawāb al-'A'māl*, (Arabic). Manshūrāt al-Riḍā. (Arabic). Qum, 1990

Al-Ṣadūq *'Ilāl al-Sharāyi'*. Second Edition, (Arabic). The Haidariya Library (Arabic). Najaf, 1966.

Al-Ṣadūq, *Man Lā Yaḥḍuruh al-Faqīh*. Comments by A.A. Qhafari,(Arabic). Manshūrāt Jāmi'ah al-Mudarrisīn fī al-Ḥawzah al-'Ilmiyyah. (Arabic). Qum, 1972.

Al-Ṣadūq, *al-Tawḥīd*, Commentry by H.H. Tehrani, (Arabic). Manshūrāt Jāmi'ah al-Mudarrisīn fī al-Ḥawzah al-'Ilmiyyah. Beirut, 1977.

Al-Ṣadūq, *al-Khiṣāl*, (Arabic). Manshūrāt Jāmi'ah al-Mudarrisīn fī al-Ḥawzah al-'Ilmiyyah. Qum, 1982.

Al-Ṣadūq, *Ma'ānī al-'Akhbār*, (Arabic). Intishārat Islamī, Qum, 1983.

Al-Ṣadūq, *'Uyūn Akhbār al-Riḍā*, Second edition. Corrections by H. Al-Ālimī, (Arabic). Manshūrāt Mu'assisah al-A'lamī li al-Maṭbū'āt, Beirut, 1984.

Al-Ṣadūq, *al-'Amālī*, (Arabic). Mu'assisah al-Bi'thah, Qum, 1996.

Scheper, S., *How to get Focussed*, First edition, Faction3. United States, 2010.

Al-Sistānī, A., *Minhāj al-Ṣāliḥīn* (Arabic). Dār al-Bathrah, Baghdad, 2009.

Shirazi, M.J., *Al-'Amthāl fī Tafsīr al-Qur'ān*. (Arabic). Dār 'Iḥyā al-Turāth al-'Arabī , Beirut, 2005

Tabatabai, M.H., *Al-Mīzān fī Tafsīr al-Qur'ān*. (Arabic). Al-'A'lamī. Beirut, 1997

Al-Ṭabrasī, F., *Makārim al-'akhlāq*, (Arabic). Maktabaat Al-Alfayn, Kuwait, 1986

Al-Ṭabrasī, F., *Majma' al-Bayān*, (Arabic). Al-'A'lamī (Arabic). Beirut, 1995.

Ibn Ṭāwūs A. Q., *Falāḥ al-Sā'il*, (Arabic). 1992, [http://shiaonlinelibrary.com], 10/02/2014

Al-Ṭayālisī, S., *Musnad Ibn Dawūd al-Ṭayālisī*, Dār al-Ma'rifah (Arabic). Beirut, 1999.

Tolle,E., *The Power of Now*, Hodder, New World Library and Namaste Publishing, Canada, 2004.

Al-Tūsī, M. *Tahdhīb al-'Aḥkām*, (Arabic). Dār al-Kutub al-Islāmīyyah. Tehran, 1997.

Yazdi, M. Comments by al-Sistānī. A. *Al-'Urwah al-Wuthqā*. (Arabic). Maktab Ayatollah al-Udhma al-Sayyid al-Sistānī. Qum, 2004.

Yazdi, P., Ahmed 'Alī, S.V., *Commentary of the Holy Qur'ān*, Islamic Mobility, [http://islamicmobility.com/elibrary_14.htm], 06/02/2014.

Zayn al-'Ābidīn, A.B., *Soaring to the Only Beloved*, Ansariyan Publications. Qum, 2004.

Websites

Forum on concentration in prayer (Arabic): [http://www.alseraj.net/cgi-bin/pros/WeeklyProblem.cgi?1&50&85ibiQigaL1149574024] 31/07/2013

Rafaat Mehdi, Methods to know Allah (swt) according to M.H. Fadlullah (Arabic): [http://arabic.bayynat.org/ArticlePage.aspx?id=2409#.Uu2LZhB_uSr] 02/02/2014

Du'ā' after prayer: [http://www.duas.org/Taqibatbaqsal.htm]. 24/09/2013

[http://www.hodaalquran.com] 15/03/2014

[http://www.al-islam.org] 15/03/2014

[http://www.shiaonlinelibrary.com] 15/03/2014

Glossary

adhān: call announcing the time of prayer

'ādāb: courtesy, manners

(as): 'alayhi al-salām/'alayhā al-salām; Peace be upon him/her

ḥādīth (pl. 'aḥādīth): the sayings (or tradition) of the Prophet (saw), the Ahl al-Bayt (as), the infallible Imāms and the companions

Ahl al-Bayt: the family of the Holy Propher which include: himself, Lady Fatema and the twelve infallible Imāms

'akhlāq: ethics, manners, attitude

'ālim: scholar, learned person

'aqīq: agate (ornamental stone)

'aṣr: afternoon

āyah (pl. āyāt): a verse in the Holy Qur'ān

bāṭil: falsehood

bismillāh: In the Name of Allah

ẓuhr: noon

du'ā': invocation, supplication, prayer

fajr: dawn

fiqīh: jurisprudence

fī sabīli Allāh: for the sake of Allah

fiṭrah: nature, disposition

ghusl: Islamic ritual bathing

ḥadīth al-qudsī: speech of Allah (swt), narrated through the Holy Prophet (saw)

ḥajj: pilgrimage of Muslims to Makkah

ḥaqq: truth

halāl: religiously lawful or allowed

harām: religiously unlawful

ḥayyah: 'make haste' (usually recited in the 'adhān and 'iqāmah)

ikhlās: sincerity

'iḥyā: revival

imām: scholar, person who leads the prayer

'īmān: faith

'inshā Allāh: Allah willing

iqāmah: opening of the prayer, a shortened form of the 'adhān

'ishā': last of the daily prayers

jamā'ah: congregation

jihād: struggle for the sake of Allah (swt)

Ka'bah: cuboid building at the centre of the sacred Mosque in Makkah

khātim: ring

khayal: imagination

khushū': submissiveness, humility, concentration in prayer

layl: night

ma'rifah: inner knowledge

madḥ: praise

makrūh: not recommended jurisprudentially

mālik: master, owner

maghrib: sunset

mu'adhdhin: the person who calls out the adhān

muṣallī: a Muslim performing the prayer

musk: a type of perfume

mustaḥab: recommended act in Islam

murāqabah: watching over

muḥāsabah: accounting

muṭma'inn: contented

nāfilah (pl. nawāfil): supererogatory prayers, recommended prayers

nafs: soul

naẓāfah: cleanliness

nūr: light

nīyyah: intention

qiblah: the direction to the Ka'bah in Makkah (which Muslims face during prayer)

qiyām: the standing position in prayer, position after ru'ku

qunūt: invocation recited during prayer after the completion of the second rak'at. Performed in the standing position with the palms of the hands raised upwards

rak'ah (pl. rak'āt): unit of prayer

rukū': the position of bowing in the prayer

(saw): sallallāhu 'alayhi wa ālih; May Allah send His salutations and blessings upon him (the Prophet) and his family

sajdah (d. sajdāt, pl. sujūd): prostration during prayer, prostration during worship

salām: greetings, peace

ṣalāh/ṣalāt (pl. ṣalawāt): Muslim's ritual prayer

sālik: a Gnostic term denoting the traveller to Allah

Shayṭān: Satan, the devil

shakk: doubt

shukr: gratitude, thanks

siwāk: teeth cleaning twig made from a twig of the Salvadora persica tree

subḥānahu wa taʿālā (swt): may He be glorified and exalted

sūrah (pl. suwar): a chapter of the Qurʿān

tafsīr: an exegesis of the Holy Qurʿān

takbīrat al-'iḥrām: saying; "*'Allāhu 'Akbar*" (Allah is Great), opening of the prayer

ṭahārah: Islamic purity

tajwīd: knowledge and application of the rules of recitation of the Holy Qurʿān

taʿqībāt: recommended duʿā' after the prayer

tasbīh (pl. tasbīhāt): glorifying and praising Allah

tashahhud: testifying the unity of Allah and Muḥammad is the Messenger of Allah, sending salutations upon Muḥammad (saw) and his family, part of the prayer while at sitting position

taslīm: the salām (greetings) with which the prayer is closed, part of the prayer while at sitting position

tawfīq: success, Allah's help

tawḥīd: believing in Allah's Oneness; monotheism

'ummah: people, nation

wuḍū: ritual ablution (made before performing the prayer)

zīyārah: visitation (usually associated with visiting the shrines of the prophet and the Ahl al-Bayt)

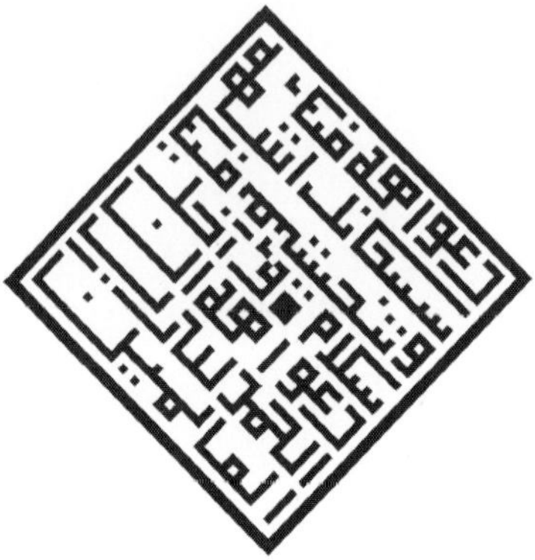

◆

Their call therein will be,
'O Allah! Immaculate are You!'
and their greeting therein will be, 'Peace!'
and their concluding call,
'All Praise belongs to Allah,
the Lord of the Words'

The Holy Qur'ān (Sūrah Yūnus, 10)